From Problem
to Possibility

From Problem to Possibility

Action and Research for Leading Up to Continuous Improvement

Mary Ann Jacobs, scc and Remigia Kushner, csj

ROWMAN & LITTLEFIELD
Lanham • Boulder • New York • London

Published by Rowman & Littlefield
An imprint of The Rowman & Littlefield Publishing Group, Inc.
4501 Forbes Boulevard, Suite 200, Lanham, Maryland 20706
www.rowman.com

86-90 Paul Street, London EC2A 4NE, United Kingdom

British Library Cataloguing in Publication Information Available

Library of Congress Cataloging-in-Publication Data Available

ISBN 9781475859744 (cloth) I ISBN 9781475859751 (pbk.) I ISBN 9781475859768 (ebook)

As we began writing this book, the world was facing a pandemic. Months of masked faces, hidden smiles, dauntless courage, closed doors, and open hearts blanketed our earth. For every heartache, at least one or more ray of sunshine prevailed. These were the everyday leaders who were leading up from problems to possibilities.

We dedicate this book to those everyday leaders—the frontline leaders in healthcare, public safety, the classroom—the unsung leaders who kept us fed, picked up our trash, provided life-saving medicine, delivered our groceries and packages, worked in local stores, cleaned our hospitals, sanitized our transit systems—the leaders at home—parents who worked remotely, tutored children, and kept the family spirit alive and well—all at the same time, children who persevered in front of different kinds of screens, our infirmed and elderly who were separated from loved ones, neighbors who kept a distant eye out for one another, those who performed multiple acts of kindness with song and dance, and the 7:00 pm clap fest to bring together those who were forced to be separated.

Most of you will probably not know about this book or find where you appear in here. But you were there—leading up from problems to possibilities. We thank you for your inspiration, your spirit, your desire for continuous improvement. You are the ones who best emanate what this book is all about!

Contents

Introduction

Everyone has problems. We all hope that they are simple problems and that plugging in the toaster will fix it when it doesn't work. But—a big but—so many problems go beyond finding the cause and fixing it. Some problems are more complex, some are actually wicked!

Now you know the three types of problems: simple, complex, wicked. Part I will tell you more about each. What you really want to know is how to solve them. Everybody wants a solution, no one wants a problem. Here's the thing—all three types need a solution. Each has a process and strategy for finding the solution. If you have problems in search of a solution, you've come to the right place! *From Problem to Possibility* looks at problems that leaders face.

Did I lose you with that sentence? You're not a leader you say? Not true if you read this book. Leaders are CEOs, that's true. Leaders are also owners of mom-and-pop stores, teachers in classrooms, parents trying to help their kids make their way through life! Leadership abounds! It is everywhere. And leaders solve problems!

So, back to simple, complex, and wicked—how do leaders at every level of an organization and life solve problems? They use the L.E.A.D.E.R. model. (All is revealed in part II.) So, if you've ever had a problem, this book will suggest some ways to use your problem as a stepping-stone to a possibility that needs a problem to imagine. You will be introduced to Theory U, how to live as though the problem has given way to the desired solution. How to engage others in helping to solve the problem. How to lead up—that is, how to take responsibility for making things better.

Dr. Jacobs developed L.E.A.D.E.R. to help school-aged youngsters—as young as kindergarten—to solve problems they brought to school with them.

Aren't you as smart as a kindergartner? Or as smart as a 5th-grader at least? You will be after you read *From Problem to Possibility.*

The authors would like to know if you were able to solve any problems using the L.E.A.D.E.R. model. Or, more importantly, if you could not. By collaborating—all of us are smarter than one of us—and using collective intelligence—chapter 3—perhaps your unsolvable problem can be a learning experience for everyone. Contact us at maryann.jacobs@manhattan.edu or send a tweet to @LeadingUp2.

Preface

When I was a principal of an elementary school, youngsters came with some problems they wanted the teacher or someone else to solve:

I forgot . . . , I can't find . . . , I don't have . . . I don't know how to . . . , I don't know what to . . .

The school took on the task of helping youngsters deal with their own problems. L.E.A.D.E.R. model was created so that kindergartners and the rest of the school would know what to do and how to do it.

When I moved on to the Superintendent's Office and then to a college teaching position, I took L.E.A.D.E.R. with me to help undergraduate teachers-to-be and new teachers develop a frame of mind that teachers need to find out how to help their future students learn better.

Action Research in the Classroom: Helping Teachers Assess and Improve Their Work was created as a guide for solving learning problems.

Invited to address doctoral candidates, and now as a college professor, I've used L.E.A.D.E.R. as the basis for the problem context and problem statement of candidates' dissertations. The potential EdDs found the presentation so helpful that they bought *Action Research in the Classroom: Helping Teachers Assess and Improve Their Work* for themselves even though the book was intended for the undergraduate teacher education candidates! Both authors thought there must be a need for L.E.A.D.E.R. for leaders!

From Problem to Possibility was written to help leaders at all levels develop a frame of mind that action research is leadership. Leaders solve problems! Leaders continuously make things better. *From Problem to Possibility: Action and Research for Leading Up to Continuous Improvement* points the way.

Part I

LEADERSHIP IS . . .

True leadership seeks continuous improvement. Leaders have the ability to turn the people in their teams into stars, people who have improved and developed their skills through the influence of their leader. In short, the definition of leadership has nothing to do with the hierarchy or position of anyone in the company; it has nothing to do with imposing views or giving orders. Rather, leaders listen to those who know or who belong to the organization. Leadership is the attitude assumed by those looking for something different, who are committed to achieving a goal and whose conviction they manage to transmit to others through enthusiasm and optimism to reach a common goal.

This part of the book examines the nature of problems and the theory of transformative leadership, how it develops, promotes group efficacy, and pursues continuous improvement to transform the organization.

Chapter 1

From Problems to Possibilities

If you have a job without problems, you don't have a job.
—Anonymous

The concept of leading up is behind solving problems to yield possibilities. Leading up has been coined to mean that individuals in the organization take responsibility for solving organizational problems by leading from the positions they have, rather than waiting for someone in charge to tell them what to do.[1] Leading up means not needing a hierarchical position to solve problems.

Leading up can be conceived of as leading up to—up to what the organization was meant to be, not returning to the past as a future possibility, but leading up to what the possibilities are for the future, taking responsibility for the success of the organization. Leading up is a possibility when all those involved in an organization in any capacity see their work as contributing to the overall purpose and meaning of the organization.

Solving problems can be a complicated process. The first step in the problem-solving process is to decide what the problem is and how the problem affects the organization and the individuals or groups of individuals in the organization. The next step is to begin at the beginning: What kind of problem is it that has to be solved?

EVERYDAY PROBLEMS, WICKED PROBLEMS, COMPLEX PROBLEMS

Everyone has problems. Organizations are no exception. Some problems are daily and annoying, some problems are serious, some problems have high-stakes consequences. Facing problems by identifying the right problem is at

3

the heart of solving problems. Covey's[2] metaphor of making sure the ladder is at the right wall points out the need to focus on the right problem before trying to solve the problem! LOOK at the problem is a basic and first step[3] to solving a problem! Part II will provide specifics about looking at the problem.

THAT WAS EASY

Some problems are simple and, as a result, are simple to solve. Simple problems are the consequence, the effect, of an obvious cause. For example, before buying a new toaster to replace one that is not doing the job it was supposed to do, troubleshooting means to check the manual, check to see that the toaster is plugged in, check that a fuse is not blown. A simple problem is usually a cause-and-effect problem. On the other hand, the simple toaster problem becomes a complicated problem if the toaster is plugged in and the fuses are ok. Now a toaster expert may be needed. Or an electrician. Or a new toaster!

If the cause of the problem is not easily discernible, the problem is more complex. If a simple problem is now a complicated problem, perhaps an expert may determine whether the problem can actually be solved. Expertise and familiarity are needed to solve a complex problem.

HOW BIG A PROBLEM IS IT?

More complex than complex problems are wicked problems! Wicked problems are large in scope. They are wicked because they represent difficulties that are social or cultural in nature. Because the wicked problem is a set of problems each of which may be the cause of other problems, finding the solution defies identifying a cause-and-effect approach or using an expert to solve the problem. While interrelatedness makes a wicked problem similar to a complex problem,[4] large, wicked problems also have large consequences.

At the time of this writing, a wicked worldwide pandemic is occurring. The problems of the pandemic in one location or state or country are similar to but different from the way the pandemic exhibits itself in another location. The successful solution in one location or state or country may be elusive in another.

It may be better to think of improving selected situations caused by wicked problems rather than trying to find solutions to wicked problems. When a vaccine is found to protect against the pandemic, another wicked problem will exist: Who will have access to the vaccine? What political issues will determine the distribution of the vaccine? What international difficulties—or worse—will arise based on the inequities of vaccine distribution? In what ways will suffering increase for what groups caused by the distribution of the vaccine?

Explanations of wicked problems lend themselves to blaming, finger-pointing, scapegoating because the problems are, well, wicked. There are no common strategies to apply. Solving some part of the problem may even exacerbate another part of the problem. Traditional problem-solving methods, even those requiring teamwork and collaboration, may be insufficient for wicked problems. Wicked problems that are social and cultural will require interdisciplinary collaboration, insight from viewpoints based on the many ways the wicked problem affects others—socially, financially, culturally, in terms of health, disease, nutrition, and the like.

THE SOLUTION IS THE PROBLEM

The wicked problem that is COVID defies a cause-and-effect solution. As of this writing, the solution has been major shutdowns, wearing masks, social distancing. The solution is the problem: What about the right to freedom of choice and movement? What about mothers not being able to go to work because they would have to leave their children? What about the education children are missing? What about allowing the government to tell citizens what to do? What about the danger to others when distancing and wearing masks are not accepted? A wicked problem indeed!

A possible solution is a vaccine. The solution may be a problem. The problem with that solution has already surfaced: Who gets the vaccine? What will whole countries do to get the vaccine? To what extent will there be boot-legged vaccines? Who and how will those most in need be taken advantage of by those who thrive on others' misfortunes and problems?

The case of pain killers is another example of a wicked problem with a solution that is a problem! The solution was pain management medication. The problem with the solution was pain management medication, with its characteristic habit-forming dependency. For wicked problems, sometimes the solution is the problem.

NOT EASY, BUT NOT WICKED

Between easy-to-solve everyday problems and sometimes insoluble wicked problems are problems more familiar to those who work in business, economics, education, health care, or have families. Those are complex problems. The goal of dealing with a complex problem is the same as the goal for an everyday problem—the goal is to find a solution. The solution is not easily based on cause-and-effect, even when an expert is consulted to help determine the cause of the effect. Like wicked problems, complex problems have interrelated parts that require interaction to reach a solution. Such interaction must have a base of teamwork and group efficacy to solve complex problem.

Working together to solve a large problem takes work, not just from large groups, but from those with large worldviews. These problem-solvers think about the possibilities posed by the problem and the possible problems posed by the solution. Minds with a large worldview think about the unthinkable—What might the consequences be? What problems might the solution cause? And who can think through the consequences to minimize a new set of unknown problems and, instead, maximize the possibilities?

WHO KNEW AND WHO KNOWS?

The description and solution of a complex problem are also complex in some of the same ways a wicked problem is complex. A problem is complex if it involves multiple goals or many possible actions that can be taken to arrive at a solution. Possible solutions may have unpredictable and unintended consequences, especially if the solutions need to be done in a fluid changing environment.[5] Based on their research, Fischer and team undertook to define Complex Problem-Solving (CPS) by disaggregating the terms of CPS.

Complexity refers to the number of elements of the system in question. The more elements there are to the issue, the more the elements are interrelated. Think of poor customer relations in a business. Is the issue related to the quality of the product? Or its price? Or is it lack of service by staff? Is it the inefficiency of how business is conducted? What has to be fixed? Just one of the elements? Fix it with the silver bullet strategy? Or, should several elements of the problem be dealt with at one time? Fix it using the shoot-with-buckshot strategy? Should all the elements underlying the problem be dealt with all at once by eliminating the entire situation? Fix it by extinguishing the problem? Or deal with none of them? Fix it by ignoring it and hoping it will go away? One problem, many elements, many possible actions to take.

A *problem* exists when there is a desired goal with no clear means of reaching the goal, when what-is and what-is-desired may be separated by a large gap because knowledge is lacking, or the means to solve the problem is lacking, or clarity about the desired end state may be lacking. *Problem-solving* then refers to a searching for a strategy or series of strategies to move from what-is, the actual state of affairs, to what-is-desired, the goal state.

Using these three definitions, Professor Fischer's team developed a strategy for working with complex problems. CPS comprises its own body of study. Professor Fischer and his team traced CPS back to the 1970s when problems arose of limits to growth, global warming, the oil crisis, failure of large businesses and banks, threat of nuclear disaster, pandemics—SARS, AIDS, Ebola, Swine flu, and other variants of the virus. It became obvious that human problem-solving had to be improved to avoid the consequences of complex problems that existed then and that continue to exist.

Even though complex problems can seem large and insurmountable, complex problems exist locally as well. Complex problems are normal for businesses with concerns about customer relations or about low profitability; citizens with issues of community health, housing, and safety; parents with concerns about their children outside the home; employers facing employee dissatisfaction, low morale, and low productivity; schools with low student achievement.

HOW TO GET OUT OF COMPLEX PROBLEMS

Dealing with local complex problems may be served by Fischer's approach to solving complex problems. Based on the team's understanding that there are multiple goals and multiple approaches for dealing with complex problems, those working to solve a complex problem had to take several steps before actually arriving at a solution to the problem. But, don't forget, complex problems may have more than one solution! Fischer and the team believed an important goal of CPS was to examine what is known about the problem, then to acquire knowledge about the problem, and then to apply that knowledge by designing a strategy to deal with the problem.

Trying to solve a complex problem is like looking in a rear-view mirror: What caused the problem? What happened then? Why did the system fail? On the other hand, considering the solution instead of the problem is like looking at a roadmap: Where is the journey leading? What is the intended destination? What is the best way to get to the destination? The irony of the rear-view mirror approach—in Einstein's words—is that a problem cannot be solved at the same level of consciousness that created it! Another irony is that a problem is almost necessary to conceive of a possible solution, a possible end goal, a possible future condition without the problem.

To arrive at the desired end goal, solving complex problems depends on collaboration to identify the problem, not only by outsiders looking in but also by those affected by the problem, and knowing how they are affected by the problem. An interim goal is knowing the desired end goal in the perceptions of those affected by the problem.

Because a complex problem is a problem for others, others are needed to solve a complex problem. Including others to collaborate as problem-solvers requires a commitment to making things better, to continuous improvement of the organization, to leading up. The commitment is the constant re-creation and transformation of the organization into what it claims to be and wants to be—profitable, effective, useful—for customers, stakeholders, employees, and constituents—who are committed to leading up!

SOLVING COMPLEX PROBLEMS

Collaboration, a trajectory toward continuous improvement, and the will to transform the organization characterize CPS. Complex problems of finance, personnel, slow growth or no growth, inefficiency, ineffectiveness, disenfranchisement of customers, or stakeholders or employees need solutions! The collective intelligence required to solve complex problems refers to shared or group intelligence that emerges from the collaboration and the collective efforts of many individuals. Decision-making by consensus requires collective intelligence. Synergy is a goal and a process that results in individuals' intelligence contributed to solving complex problems. Collective intelligence uses individual intelligence to learn from solutions that do not work and do not solve the problem.

Simply put, collective intelligence is a group's knowledge. When groups work together, they create intelligence beyond what can be created individually. Synergy results—the whole is greater than the sum of the parts. Pierre Lévy[6] defined collective intelligence as a form of distributed intelligence that is constantly enhanced. The result is skill put into action in a way that also recognizes others and, where possible, enriches individuals. Collective intelligence thus enhances social knowledge and expands human interactions.

When collective intelligence is applied, it shifts knowledge and power from an individual problem-solver, often someone who holds a hierarchical position. The shift that takes place is to the efficacy of the group that believes in leading up. Education is a good example of the shift from individual learning to collective learning. Based on the opportunities now available to participate in knowledge production, in MOOCs, for example, micro-credentialing, badges, and other means and modes of learning outside formal brick and mortar settings, it is no longer necessary to rely solely on the bricks and mortar enterprises to acquire learning and credentials.

The intelligence needed to adapt and solve problems, to reason, learn, and predict are aspects of collective intelligence and capacity. Strategically using facts that have been gathered is another crucial component of collective intelligence. Collective intelligence is largely collaborative work of a group working together to accomplish a common goal. With collaboration, collective learning is possible because individuals share what they learned. Their work produces the collective intelligence that shifts control and dispensing of information from individuals to groups—neighbors in a neighborhood, workers in a company, members of a professional organization.

Collective intelligence describes how group intellect begins to form when people work together. The group shares information and collectively solves problems, giving the group a greater chance to find answers than they would have on working individually. The reason this works is because the crowd achieves wisdom by finding a consensus in correct answers and by dismissing or discarding incorrect or deviant ideas. Collective intelligence is needed to solve complex problems with its variety of interrelationships.

A characteristic of collaborative work that produces collective intelligence is the presence of a group leader. The leader in a collaborative group may be a formal leader—the principal investigator of a research study, for example. The collaborative group leader might also be appointed or responsible for the productivity of the group. Sometimes the leader in a collaborative group is an informal leader—someone with an idea or suggestion that is seen as reasonable or useful by others.

Whether the collaborating group has a formal or informal leader, the fact that there is a leader in a collaborative or cooperative group leads to considering the leadership of the whole. What kind of leadership is needed so collaborative problem-solving becomes the norm rather than the exception? What kind of leader encourages leadership in cooperative groups? How does the appointed, hierarchical leader participate in the creation of group intelligence and solutions to complex problems? That is the next question: What kind of leadership allows leading up? What kind of leadership encourages and enhances the collective intelligence that produces possibilities from complex problems?

WHAT KIND OF LEADERSHIP?

The leader's job is to fix it! Solve the problem! Make things better! Leaders solve problems. True leadership, leadership that is more than a position, seeks constantly to make the organization better. Leaders can turn the people in their teams into stars, into people who have improved and developed their skills through the influence of the leader. In short, the work and function of leadership has nothing to do with the hierarchical position of anyone in the company; it has nothing to do with imposing views or giving orders. Rather, leaders listen to those who belong to the organization. Leadership is the attitude assumed by those committed to achieving a goal. Leaders manage to transmit to others the enthusiasm and optimism needed to reach a common goal.

Increased collaboration, a more radical inclusion, and a greater commitment to lifelong learning are poised to change the future of work. Inam's conception of The Fourth Industrial Revolution[7] (4IR) will require leaders, particularly in key decision-making roles, to evolve mindsets, skill sets, values, and behaviors if all are to thrive in disruptive times. The caveat is that leadership is not a position! Leadership is action. Those who want to make work better, service better, clients, customers, stakeholders, children, students better are leaders, with or without a bureaucratic or hierarchical position.

When Google is asked, "What is leadership?" there are 5,640,000,000 results in just about a half minute. Asked how many definitions of leadership there are, ResearchGate answers with a list of over 200 definitions of leadership that include inspiration, a journey, an action, a position; shared, mission-centered, visionary, motivating, collaborative, informative, service; position, bureaucratic, democratic, sharing, protective, optimistic, future centered, realistic, imaginative.

Warren Bennis[8] studied leadership and believed that "Of all the hazy and confounding areas in social psychology, leadership theory undoubtedly contends for the top nomination. And, ironically, probably more has been written and less known about leadership than about any other topic in the behavioral sciences." James MacGregor Burns[9] likewise believed that "Leadership is one of the most observed and least understood phenomena on earth." The problem of understanding leadership arises not only in the enactment of leadership theory but also in the definition of leadership. Stogdill claimed that "There are almost as many definitions of leadership as [there are] those who have attempted to define the concept."[10]

What an elusive ubiquitous topic! The contradiction is intentional. A leader can be inspirational or a task-master, a visionary or a maintainer of the status quo, a servant or a placeholder in a bureaucracy, a facilitator of others' work or a protector of a position. How can there be so much choice about what leadership is? The answer depends on the definition. Leaders are CEOs of hospitals, mega-corporations, and start-up companies. Leaders also take charge of mom-and-pop stores, sewing circles, clubs, families, and themselves! Even if the corporation has many members, the followers of the leader do not comprise the entire organization. There is leadership within the groups that exist in organizations. The leaders within groups still remain subordinates of the CEO. It is through the followership of middle managers, leaders within groups, the CEO leads the organization.

What if there are no followers, how can there be a leader? Every leader leads a party of at least one, that is, self! Leading self is not a joke. If a party of one cannot be led, how can the leadership of others be possible? "Do as I say, not as I do," "Because I said so" "Because I am the boss!" said literally or figuratively simply does not work! Compliance without commitment has unintended consequences that include ennui, indifference, low morale, high absenteeism, poor customer service, and on and on.

Some organizations count on the fact that individuals cannot make the commitment to lead self, to keep promises made to themselves. How many sign up for a gym membership as a New Year resolution? CreditDonkey's statistics indicate that 80 percent of those who sign up for a gym membership in January will stop attending within five months; 14 percent will quit before February.[11] Leading self is the *sine qua non* of leadership.

Effective leaders have effective problem-solving strategies that go beyond "I will take care of it!" CPS requires collaboration and interaction that transform followers into participants, participants into leaders. Participants do not take over leadership of the organization, but they do lead in an area of expertise that they possess or by the investment they have in a potential solution, or by their ability to see possibilities provided by the end goal.

Leading up requires a commitment to the organization in such a way that the goals of the individual and the goals of the organization are served. Leading up means taking responsibility for the organization and leading from the position one has, rather than needing a hierarchical position to do so. Leading up means leading up to—up to what the organization was meant to be, what the organization can be, what the possibilities are for the organization. Leading up is diametrically opposed to returning to the past as a future possibility. Instead, leading up means leading to future possibilities for all those involved in the organization in any capacity.

NASA decided to transform itself by infusing the organization's mission into every activity of the organization. The floor mopper was not mopping the floor, "I'm sending a man to the moon!"[12] "I'm not laying bricks, I am building a cathedral."[13] The leader's role is transformative—transforming followers into participants; participants into leaders. The effective leader helps participants transform complaint into commitment, blame into responsibility.[14]

Though the process might seem mysterious, the effective leader provides an environment for solving complex problems. That environment includes time for personal and collective reflection, cognitive processing to initiate creative problem-solving and thinking imaginatively, and, where possible, seeking the simplicity behind the complexity.

Problem-solvers are not necessarily geniuses; they sometimes think their way through problems. Problem-solvers see past problems and focus instead on challenges, opportunities, and possibilities. They are able to distinguish symptoms and problems. They have nurtured a will to learn and a will to act on what they have learned.

It is not enough for a leader to solve a problem that exists. The leader has to look for a problem that has not come up yet. Abraham Lincoln did just that. After he won the Republican Party nomination that made him president, he did not simply figure out what to do about the problem of slavery. He anticipated the problem that might come up when his rivals who lost the election took their important political places. In a *Team of Rivals*, Doris Kearns Goodwin presented Abraham Lincoln as the leader who anticipated problems that he would have to solve.[15] He got in front of the problems by surrounding himself with those most likely to criticize and undermine his presidential behavior—his rivals who competed with him for the presidency.

With their insight and perceptions that were different from his, he created a wrap-around problem-solving strategy. Churchill solved problems by facing them head-on. When a problem surfaced, he stood up to it—"Never give in! Never give in!"[16] Gandhi stood firm and by his example inspired others to take a beating when necessary. Mother Teresa was so clear about the problem that she spent a lifetime dealing with it and ultimately extended her motivation inspiring action beyond the poor of India.

Their will to act means acting in the present on a future goal. Senge, Scharmer, Jaworski, and Flowers called this leadership stance *presencing*.[17] Sharmer went on with Kaufer to describe presencing as pre-sensing what the future will require and acting from the future goal rather than from the present state of affairs.[18] The will to act on future possibilities means transforming problems into a gateway to a future rather than a return to the past that produced the problem in the first place. Presencing is transformative leadership. The qualities and characteristics of transformational leadership are needed to lead up from problems to possibilities.

NOTES

1. Leading Up. (2015, November 3). *The Collaborative Way®*. https://collaborativeway.com/general/leading-up/

2. Covey, S. (2004). *Seven habits of highly effective people: Powerful lessons in personal change*. Free Press.

3. Jacobs, M. A. and Cooper, B. (2016). *Action research in the classroom: Helping teachers improve their craft*. Rowman and Littlefield.

4. Walls, A. J. (2020, January 29). Wicked design and a new model for complex problem-solving. *Medium*. https://medium.com/swlh/wicked-design-and-a-new-model-for-complex-problem-solving-116bfb832d4d

5. Fischer, A., Grieff, S., and Funke, J. (Winter 2012). The process of solving complex problems. *The Journal of Problem Solving* 4(1), 19–42. doi: 10.7771/1932-6246.1118.

6. Nielsen, M. (2010, May 23). *Collective intelligence by Pierre Levy*. https://michaelnielsen.org/blog/collective-intelligence-by-pierre-levy/

7. Inam, H. (2020, January 31). Leadership must change to match the future of work. *SmartBrief*. https://www.smartbrief.com/branded/F6D8DF94-3AEB-4A28 -8343-BDDAF6341D54/B0E22C7B-F4AA-4E6E-A132-B4832645B26E

8. Bennis, W. (1959, December). Leadership theory and administrative behavior: The problem of authority. *Administrative Science Quarterly 4*(3), 259–301.

9. McManus, R. (2016, December 6). Understanding leadership, one of the most misunderstood phenomena. *Engage*. https://www.claremontlincoln.edu/engage/ethical-leadership/understanding-leadership-misunderstood/

10. Shaver, E. (2014, July 18). The many definitions of leadership. *Medical Technology Innovator*. https://www.ericshaver.com/the-many-definitions-of-leadership

11. Lake, R. (2014, December 29). 23 gym membership statistics that will astound you. *CreditDonkey*. https://www.creditdonkey.com/gym-membership-statistics.html

12. Carton, A. M. (2018). I'm not mopping floors, I'm putting a man on the moon: How NASA leaders enhanced the meaningfulness of work by changing the meaning of work. *Administrative Science Quarterly, 63*(2), 323–369. doi: 10 1177/00 01839217713748

13. Kukolic, S. (2017, Oct. 19). Are you laying bricks or building a cathedral? *HuffPost*. https://www.huffpost.com/entry/are-you-laying-bricks-or-_b_12387634

14. Kagan, R. & Lahey, L. L. (2001). *Seven languages for transformation: How the way we talk can change the way we work*. Jossey-Bass.

15. Kearns-Goodwin, D. (2005). *A team of rivals: The political genius Abraham Lincoln*. Simon and Schuster Paperbacks.

16. International Churchill Society. (2009, May 6). *Quotes*. https://winston-churchill.org/resources/reference/frequently-asked-questions/quotes-faq-2/#:~:text= %E2%80%9CThis%20is%20the%20lesso

17. Senge, P., et al. (2004). *Presence: Exploring profound change in people, organizations, and society*. Doubleday.

18. Scharmer, O. and Kaufer, K. (2013). *Leading from the emerging future: From ego-system to eco-system economies*. Berrett-Koehler.

Chapter 2

Transformational Leadership

*Transformational leaders don't start by denying the world around them.
Instead, they work to create the future world they would like to live in.*
—*Godin*

Leadership in this chapter will be presented as Transformational Leadership, a theory of leadership whereby a leader works with teams to identify needed change, creates a vision to guide the change, and executes the change in partnership with committed members of the organization. Transformational leadership in this chapter will be defined as a leadership approach that causes a change in individuals and social systems, creates valuable and positive change in the followers with the end goal of developing followers into leaders, enhances the motivation, morale, and performance of followers by transcending the follower's wants and needs to the mission and a sense of the collective identity of the organization. The transformational leader is the role model for followers and inspires them, challenges them to take greater ownership of improvement through a sense of group efficacy.[1]

LEADING SELF, LEADING OTHERS, AND
LEADING THE ORGANIZATION

Toward the end of the 1970s, transformational leadership theory emerged. James McGregor Burns in his 1978 book *Leadership*[2] described this theory as a process whereby "leaders and their followers raise one another to higher levels of morality and motivation." Further development of this theory by Bernard Bass (1985) described transformational leaders as models of integrity and fairness who set goals, had high expectations, encouraged, supported, and recognized others, and moved people to surpass their own personal best. Transformational leadership is still regarded as one of the most important ideas in leadership.

The transformational leader is a role model for the members of the organization. Being a role model requires knowledge, skill, and dispositions toward leading self, a prerequisite to leading others. Leading self is personal mastery, the beginning of the journey to organizational transformation. By leading self, then by leading others to lead themselves (make leaders of followers), and then by leading with others, organizational transformation is possible.

Knowing how and having the skill to lead self are the basic knowledge at the micro-level of leadership. The goal is not just self-awareness, but also executive functioning that provides the impetus for planning and emotional control. Leading self means choosing to see the half-full glass, believing that thoughts are things.[3] Other dispositions for leading self include taking a proactive stance toward a goal; a frame of mind that change is inevitable but that growth is optional; that being a victim is a choice; and that power is not a four-letter word (p. 16).

Leading others to lead themselves is a hallmark of transformational leaders. Making leaders of followers in Burns' words means realizing that leaders cannot make anyone do anything. When followers comply and possibly perform even though they disagree, it may be because they want to avoid something else or get something based on their self-interest. The transformational leader is disposed to Goethe's axiom that if we treat people as they are, they will remain so. If we treat them as they might be, they will become so.[4]

While external supervision may correct errors, the leader realizes that only internal supervision can prevent errors. Internal supervision is required for commitment. This commitment to preventing errors leads to leading up—accepting the responsibility for the continuous improvement of the organization. Followers also lead self. Followers become leaders. These leadership dispositions, coupled with the skill to make them active, pave the way for working with others to transform the organization.

The skills and dispositions for leading the organization include the realization that all change begins with a change of mind;[5] that relationships are all there is[6] with internal and external customers. Making change happen applies skills to enact the disposition that information is to the organization what blood is to the body and that participation in the life of the organization is an ethical imperative.[7]

The transformational leader has the capacity to distinguish difficult people and situations from conflict—real conflict, the conflict that deserves the name. True conflict exposes values at opposite ends of the continuum. The leader's job is not to manage, control, eliminate, forestall, diffuse, or reduce conflict. Instead, the leader's job is to develop a process to find the values inherent in the conflict.

COMMUNICATE TO INSPIRE

The transformational leader believes communication through the organization functions like blood in the human body. When blood is healthy and flows freely, all parts of the body function effectively. When communication flows freely, the organization can also function properly and effectively. But, just as a blockage of blood can sometimes damage the body, so too a blockage in communication—who has a right to know, not needed at your level, dismissing questions, patronizing responses—damages the organization.

To be heard, the leader must listen first, that is, must listen to others' thinking. After all, perception of the truth or of reality may not be true or real at all. Claudel says it this way: Truth has nothing to do with the number of people it convinces. The leader must realize that others will not have a leader's perspective or perception. So, leaders should not believe everything they think.[8] Listening generously means using mouth and ears in proportion to their existence. Everyone has two ears and only one mouth for a reason.

If what is said is not what is heard, it is not the listener's problem. The burden of communication is on the person with the message. The responsibility for communication is accompanied by the need to repeat, to use different words, to hear back from the listener if the intended message is the message that was received.

A difficult perception for the leader to overcome is that those in a hierarchical position and those in the position of doing the work of the organization speak different languages. While this is an organizational necessity, there must be some common language to improve the organization. There must be a common vision and purpose that the members of the organization know, believe, and act to achieve. Communication is the key to communication that inspires.

CREATING A DESIRED FUTURE
FOR THE ORGANIZATION

As Henry Kissinger noted: "The task of the leader is to get his people from where they are to where they have not been."[9] Vision, mission, and power together give strength to others so that they may stand on their own. The leader's task, challenge, and responsibility are to create the conditions that will produce in the future what is lacking in the present.[10] Leading up means leading the organization to a future that fulfills the promise of the mission and vision of the organization. Mission and vision become the driving forces of the transformational leader and the members of that organization.

The well-known biblical admonition of Proverbs 29:18, that "without vision, the people perish," points to the need for some source of guidance. For some Christians, the proverb points to the need for leaders to be guided by a focus, a destination, a goal for the journey. Some of the sources of leadership point to the need for vision. Bass believed that transformational leadership required sharing the vision and occurred when "leaders broaden and elevate the interests of their employees, when they generate awareness and acceptance of the purposes and mission of the group, and when they stir their employees to look beyond their own self-interest for the good of the group."[11]

In a simple form, vision is a mental picture of something that has not yet occurred but is hoped for. Its power lies in what is hoped for.

The internet is replete with stories of successful grand failures that illustrate the power of vision: Walt Disney was fired from a newspaper because he "lacked imagination and had no good ideas."[12] Oprah Winfrey, at the age of 22, was fired from her job as a television reporter because she was "unfit for TV."[13] Steven Spielberg was rejected from film school, not once, not twice, but three times. Michael Jordan was cut from his high-school basketball team. Thomas Edison failed some 10,000 times before successfully inventing the light bulb. How is it, then, that they are known for the very things at which they *failed*?

Jim Carrey wrote himself a $10 million check that he postdated by ten years. He was able to cash that check. Mary Higgins Clark had her books rejected forty times in the 50s. In the 90s, she cashed a check for $64 million. James Joyce's epic masterpiece *Ulysses*, regarded as one of the greatest Irish novels, was repeatedly rejected by baffled publishers before finally being published in a tiny edition in Paris in 1922 by his friend Sylvia Beach's Shakespeare & Co bookshop; a copy of the first edition sold a few years ago for £275,000. J. K. Rowling posted her initial rejections; in 2010, long after she came off the dole, she was listed among the world's wealthiest women.

Max DePree[14] reminded us that the signs of outstanding leadership appear primarily among the followers. It sounds like the followers determine the leader. There is a cartoon showing someone running to catch up with a crowd of people running ahead. The caption reads: *I have to follow them! I am their leader!* A bit humorous, but a kernel of truth nonetheless. Leading *with* others becomes the moral imperative, to transform the organization into more of what it is intended to be. And the organization is made up of people, not only of spreadsheets or strategic plans!

The transformational leader leads from future possibilities. Scharmer's Theory U (2018) represents acting as though the future has been enacted in the present. His theory is based on a concept he calls "presencing"—a blend of the words *presence* and *sensing*. He describes this as a heightened sense of attention that requires individuals and groups to listen, observe, sense, and pre-sense, crystallize, learn by doing, and allow group members to lead up—to act as leaders invested in the organization. When that shift happens, people begin to operate from a future space of possibility that they feel wants to emerge.[15]

Leading up depends on the capacity to see problems as possibilities, as gateways to the desired future instead of focusing on the problem and its causes that may only extend the past. The transformational leader models presencing. Leading up requires seeing what has not yet occurred, seeing the desired future on the other side of the problem, the future that will emerge by using the problem as a gateway to what could be.[16] Leading up is a transcendent activity. As such, the problem becomes a steppingstone to act as though something better already exists. When other members join that commitment, a sense of efficacy develops, a sense that the future possibility exists because the members can make it so.

Leading up to make a future possibility a reality can function as the hub of a wheel. The wheel is the community that forms the spokes and rim. The parts of the wheel move together. The individuals who are part of the wheel make their contributions to the future interdependently. Interdependence facilitates the group's sense of efficacy, makes presencing possible—living in a future as it emerges. Members participate in what the leader models—generous listening, seeing things in a similar way, seeking to know more, leading self, accepting leadership. Attention and intention are focused on what could be rather than on what-is. Followers become leaders, and the organization learns.

ENACTING ORGANIZATIONAL TRANSFORMATION

The leading self process continues by leading others to lead themselves—turning followers into leaders. Achieving organizational transformation means working with other leaders for the continuous improvement of the organization. Organizational transformation means the organization becomes more of what it claims in its vision and mission statements, in its promise to its stakeholders. It does so by learning to develop critical organizational competencies and improving processes to develop those competencies.

On-going learning by all the members of the organization forms the building blocks of the learning organization. Building the learning organization requires a commitment to the vision and mission, espoused to be the basis of organizational transformation. This espoused theory forms the underpinning of action[17] that includes internal and external stakeholders in the organization.

The knowledge, skills, and dispositions of leaders at all levels of the organization facilitate necessary and valuable changes in the organization. Enacting successful change becomes the impetus for further action in favor of the organizational change. Constant focus on the mission and vision of the organization is required so members' perceptions can be congruent, so their actions are in favor of the desired development of the organization.

The leader's responsibility thus extends to managing perceptions and focusing on the future good of the organization, on the organization's responsibility to stakeholders, on keeping the organization's promises. Leading up by all members of the organization requires their intention to be effective, their ability to lead self, their focus on what the organization can be and must be to exist into the future.

The differences in hierarchical leadership and transformational leadership impact the culture, morale, and success of an organization. Hierarchical and bureaucratic leadership is just one of many styles of leadership available to the leader of an organization. It is incumbent on the leader to understand the effect of leadership style on the organization and its members.

The identifying characteristics of leadership styles point to the type of relationships and effect the style will have. For example, observable characteristics of transformational leadership are innovation, empathy, and inspiration. The characteristics of the transactional leader on the other hand are based on regimentation, accomplishment-focus, and efficiency.

Democratic and autocratic leadership styles display opposing characteristics. Democratic leads with active engagement, supportive and accountable leadership while autocratic leads by a disciplined, decisive, and confident leader. Other leadership styles include situational which is characterized as agile, adaptable, versatile; laissez-faire is open-minded, trusting, communicative; charismatic is inspiring, influential, personally invested, and cross-cultural is inclusive, respectful, versatile.

Nothing in the presentation of the characteristics has a negative connotation. Leaders need to be aware of the consequences and effects of the leadership style they choose. An autocratic style may be just right with newcomers, inexperienced members of the organizations, trainees for a specific function. Laissez-faire characteristics may be needed by those with already established skill for their work or for those with many years of experience at their jobs.

What is important is that leaders know the effects of their leadership styles and characteristics. Do those characteristics move the organization forward? Does leadership behavior enhance or hinder the commitment and engagement of followers? Does the leader's style encourage and enhance leading up so that continuous improvement is a reality? Does the group think it?

What leadership style contributes to the group's belief that they can make the organization better?

What kind of leader is mission-driven, sees time as producing something tangible, is focused on problems as possibilities, has a will to learn and a will to act? Leaders choose.[18]

NOTES

1. Burns, J. M. (2003). *Transforming leadership: A new pursuit of happiness.* Atlantic Monthly Press.

2. Bass, B. M. (1985). *Leadership and performance beyond expectation.* New York: Free Press.

3. Jacobs, M. A. and Kushner, S. R. (2017). *How can you become the boss: From personal mastery to organizational transformation.* Rowman and Littlefield.

4. von Goethe, J. W. (n.d.). *A quote by Johann Wolfgang von Goethe.* (n.d.). Goodreads. https://www.goodreads.com/quotes/7918578-if-we-treat-people-as-they-are-we-make-them

5. Covey, S. R. (1991). *The seven habits of highly effective people.* Provo, UT: Covey Leadership Center.

6. Wheatley, M. (1997). Goodbye, command and control. *Leader to Leader, 1997*(3), 21–28.

7. Jacobs and Kushner, *How can you become the boss?*

8. Lokos, A. (2010). *Pocket peace: Effective practices for enlightened living.* Penguin Books.

9. The leader's task—History moments. (2014, October 16). *History Moments Blog.* https://historyweblog.com/2014/10/the-leaders-task/

10. Kushner, S. R. (1982). *Action theory congruence and the exercise of transformational leadership in Catholic elementary schools.* Fordham Research Commons. https://research.library.fordham.edu/dissertations/AAI8223606

11. Bass, B. M. (Winter 1990). Transactional to transformational leadership: Learning to share the vision. *Organizational Dynamics, 18*(21).

12. These five business icons got fired before they became legends. *The Economic Times.* https://economictimes.indiatimes.com/these-five-business-icons-got-fired-before-they-became-legends/articleshow/46549923.cms?from=mdr

13. "Oprah Winfrey was told she was 'unfit' for TV news." https://aplus.com/v/85643/oprah-winfrey-was-told-she-was-unfit-for-tv-news/

14. de Pree, M. (1990) *Leadership is an art.* Doubleday

15. Scharmer, O. (2018). *The essentials of Theory U: Core principles and applications.* Berrett-Koehler Publishers, 2018.

16. Scharmer, *The essentials of Theory U.*

17. Argyris & Schon (1978).

18. Boogaard, K. (2019, January 23). 8 common leadership styles (and how to find yours). *The Muse.* https://www.themuse.com/advice/common-leadership-styles-with-pros-and-cons

REFERENCES

Bass, B. M. (Winter, 1990). Transactional to transformational leadership: Learning to share the vision. *Organizational Dynamics, 18*(3), 19–31.

Boogaard, K. (2019, January 23). 8 common leadership styles (and how to find yours). *The Muse.* https://www.themuse.com/advice/common-leadership-styles-with-pros-and-cons

Burns, J. M. (2003). *Transforming leadership: A new pursuit of happiness.* Atlantic Monthly Press

Covey, S. R. (1991). *The seven habits of highly effective people.* Covey Leadership Center.

de Pree, M. (1990) *Leadership is an art.* Doubleday.

Jacobs, M. A. and Kushner, S. R. (2017). *How can you become the boss: From personal mastery to organizational transformation.* Rowman and Littlefield.

Kushner, S. R. (1982). *Action theory congruence and the exercise of transformational leadership in Catholic elementary schools.* Fordham Research Commons. https://research.library.fordham.edu/dissertations/AAI8223606

Lokos, A. (2010). *Pocket peace: Effective practices for enlightened living.* Penguin Books.

Oprah Winfrey was told she was 'unfit' for TV news. https://aplus.com/v/85643/oprah-winfrey-was-told-she-was-unfit-for-tv-news/

Scharmer, O. (2018). *The essentials of Theory U: Core principles and applications.* Berrett-Koehler.

The leader's task. (2014, October 16). *History Moments Blog.* https://historyweblog.com/2014/10/the-leaders-task/

These five business icons got fired before they became legends. *The Economic Times.* https://economictimes.indiatimes.com/these-five-business-icons-got-fired-before-they-became-legends/articleshow/46549923.cms?from=mdr

von Goethe, J. W. (n.d.). *A quote by Johann Wolfgang von Goethe.* (n.d.). Goodreads. https://www.goodreads.com/quotes/7918578-if-we-treat-people-as-they-are-we-make-them

Wheatley, M. (1997). Goodbye, command and control. *Leader to Leader, 1997*(3), 21–28.

Chapter 3

Group Efficacy

All of Us Is Smarter Than One of Us

When the best leader's work is done the people say, We did it ourselves!
—*Lao Tzu*

The leader's work is the continuous improvement of the organization. The transformational leader collaborates with others to transform the organization and to transform followers into leaders. Followers can be informal leaders of groups within the organization. Like the work of the leader of the organization, the group's work is to complete a task or improve a process or improve their own work. Working for the continuous improvement of the organization is collaboration in organizational transformation.

Informal leadership of small groups has been studied to find out if an informal leader can influence or persuade group members to accept the responsibility to improve the organization—to lead up. If the informal group leader believed the group could accomplish the task and meet the goal, it was also likely that the group would also believe they could accomplish the task. If the members of the group believed they could do what needs to be done, group efficacy was the result.

Individuals have to think they can, and if the group thinks it can, then group efficacy will contribute to the goal of making the organization better. Group efficacy is extrapolated from Bandura's theory of self-efficacy,[1] the belief that individuals can solve problems and make improvements in their lives. Group—or collective—efficacy transfers that belief or conviction from the individual to the group. The individuals in the group believe that their work together will be effective, they are convinced that they can make a difference.

Researchers have measured group efficacy to find out how group efficacy begins and develops, have examined the part individuals' perceptions of efficacy play in the group's efficacy, and tried to find out if group efficacy can be measured. Gibson[2] looked for a way to predict group efficacy by having the group discuss their estimate of the time needed to complete a task. Gibson's study found that if the group knew its task, and discussed with each how long the task might take, then the results of the group's work were somewhat predictable. The group seemed able to complete the task before them.

Pescosolido[3] studied informal leadership of small groups to learn whether the informal leader of a group could have an effect on the groups' sense of efficacy. When the informal leader and group members publicly expressed their belief that the goal could be accomplished, they were able to persuade the group that their work together could achieve the goal. The informal leader did not expect group efficacy to simply exist. Instead, the informal leader and group members with a sense of efficacy needed to develop efficacy within the group.

Developing group efficacy meant providing information so the group's collective efficacy could be enhanced with information about other tasks they successfully completed. Information about the successes of other groups also helped develop group efficacy. Other helpful information from the members of the group was provided when group members expressed their willingness to participate. Their clear understanding of their role in the task (I'm not mopping a floor; I am sending a man to the moon!) helped the group develop the collective efficacy that made it possible to complete the task.

Developing group efficacy begins with self-efficacy. An individual may need to grow beyond compliance with rules and procedures. Expectations, successful performance, and task-goal settings may help an individual develop the commitment needed to persist despite difficulties. Similarly, moving from dependence on direction, rules, and procedural regulations, to a sense of responsible self-direction can lead to interdependence with the other members of the group. Individual commitment coupled with interdependence in service to a task-oriented goal can lead to organizational transformation.

Allowing group members to lead themselves to a needed result seems to point to group efficacy as a result of transformational leadership. The group develops purposeful expectations and, in that way, leads the leader with those expectations. Thus, collaborative leadership is the group's—and leader's—conviction that, together, they can make a difference. Together, they lead up!

Pescosolido[4] reminds us that group efficacy differs from self-confidence or general confidence that is an affective state, while efficacy is extremely task-specific. Group efficacy has the ability to affect a group's mission, their commitment, how the group members work together, and the group's ability to persist in the face of difficulties. Group efficacy illustrates the potential to make leaders of followers.

Pescosolido studied an example of collaborative learning and leading with a cohort of candidates for a degree who came together as a group to work toward a postgraduate degree. The cohort stayed together and built a sense of community around their research after their studies when they became practitioners. They used concepts of system thinking and learning for their continuing research because they derived benefit from working as a community on their dissertations. The group held three-hour monthly meetings to support each other, reflected as a group in conditions that produced insight. They developed new knowledge about their research processes. The cohort continued to work together with the structure and a process they formed that supported their PhD goal.

The example of the cohort focused on task points to group efficacy emerging from performing together and accomplishing something together as a group. The cohort's work also linked group efficacy with the group's productivity. The cohort's efficacy extended their group work past the PhD, continued their personal learning and development, contributed to their satisfaction with leadership opportunities, and, paradoxically, improved the ability to work independently of the cohort.

Based on their work toward a PhD for each member, the cohort developed higher levels of group efficacy, benefited from the sustainability of the group once the goal was achieved, and continued individual learning, self-development, and increased individual autonomy. The cohort's success solidified the members' belief that their collective efficacy supported their confidence, their ability to make a difference, to solve a problem, to deal with an issue. They met the goal of leading up!

The background of collective efficacy is a sociological application in the field of crime deterrence.[5] When neighbors had to deal with the complex problem of crime in their neighborhood, neighbors accepted the responsibility to do something to control the behavior of individuals and groups damaging property in the community. The solution to the complex problem of crime in the neighborhood meant controlling unwanted behavior so that neighbors could contribute to and live in a safe and orderly environment. Neighbors who believed they could, did! They solved a problem and improved their lives.

Advocates of collective efficacy saw beyond a neighborhood problem to the possibility of reducing, or even eliminating, unwanted behavior. The increased community control over individuals' behavior created an environment where violent crime was less likely to occur. Increased collective efficacy led to the possibility of a significant reduction of crime in the community.

More mundane tasks that increased collective efficacy included picking up litter and generally taking responsibility for keeping the neighborhood clean. Those efficacious activities encouraged larger improvements—removing graffiti, repairing and restoring dilapidated houses, shoveling snow for the elderly.[6]

The heroes of Black Lives Matter[7] understand collective efficacy—no one person or even a select group of persons can solve a pervasive problem. The goal is to live in the desired future. Realizing the possibility of reaching the desired goal meant identifying that goal, examining what is known about the problem by gathering perceptions and suggestions. To move from the problem toward a possible solution meant acquiring knowledge from other communities that were successful in a similar circumstance. More formal ways of acquiring knowledge were through study, consultations with law enforcement, and other experts.

Collaboratively designing a plan could extend from seeking grants to mapping out streets to setting up street-level patrols. Solving the problem needed collaboration and the sense that "we are in this together!" Together we can do something! Together, we can make things better. Hubbard tells the stories of seventeen unsung, relatively unknown heroes who believed in the possibilities they could reach.

Communities with high levels of collective efficacy have lower rates of violence and homicide, suggesting that community participation in preventing violence reduces crime. This view of collective efficacy, based on shared values, trust, and cooperation to prevent violence and crime, means that the community members can live in a safe environment. This concept may explain why urban neighborhoods differ from each other in the amount of crime that takes place in them. If neighbors monitor group behavior and are willing to intervene in fights or prevent disorder, the possibility is there for reducing violent crime.

LEADERSHIP FOR COLLECTIVE EFFICACY

The role of leadership in collective efficacy may be inferred from James MacGregor Burns (2003) interpretation of the power of a group of individuals to make a change in government policy. Describing changes in policy that FDR made, Burns developed the trajectory from the group needs to group wants to the group needing what they wanted (p. 141). The group developed purposeful expectations (p. 143) for themselves and for their leaders.

Collective efficacy grew from Bandura's theory of self-efficacy—an individual's belief in the ability to behave in a desirable way. That belief facilitated reaching a goal, improving performance, or improving a life condition.

For Bandura, self-efficacy was an individual's confidence in the ability to exert control over one's own motivation, behavior, and social environment.[8]

Self-Efficacy Theory (SET) has influenced research, education, and clinical practice especially in the field of health psychology.[9] For example, self-efficacy as a form of self-mastery has been used to modify behavior to manage chronic disease, smoking cessation, alcohol use, eating disorders, pain control, and exercise. A meta-analysis reported in PsycINFO®[10] lists investigations of self-efficacy in weight control. Other studies show the value of self-efficacy to the locus of control, sense of coherence, learned helplessness. The study of self-efficacy theory in health-related domains has encouraged its use in research addressing the prevention of HIV and lower high blood pressure as well.

A current nutrition-based weight loss program[11] advertises a psychology-based approach to changing clients' ways of thinking about how, when, and why they eat the way they do. The information provided to change clients' minds is similar to Bandura's recommended sources of information: others have done it; your coaches will share their journeys and learnings with you, you will attend meetings with others who are also committed to maintain your commitment and conviction, you will measure your wins, no matter how small. The end goal is helping each client believe "I can do this!"

This cognitive behavior and continual drive for improvement have influenced all manner of human experience, the goals for which people strive, the amount of energy expended toward goal achievement, and the likelihood of attaining particular levels of behavioral performance. Applied to group efficacy, the desired outcome has a transcendent quality—the goal attainment extends beyond service to the individual outward to the community, the product, the organization—the belief in and work toward the possibilities that problems present.

What does collective efficacy look like in action? Toyota's use of the Five Whys (2021) is an example of group efficacy applied to the goal of a better car for those who purchase a Toyota. The Five Whys process is research in action and will be presented with other examples in Part II.

Successful use of the Five Whys technique permits an informed decision. That decision is then based on insights from those affected by the problem, by what is actually happening on the work floor. A necessary component of problem-solving using the Five Whys is gathering a team to collaborate on solving a problem because the Five Whys is not an individual task. The goal is to reach a consensus about the root problem and develop a way to make things better. Five Whys is a leading-up strategy.

The many uses of the Five Whys point to constantly trying to improve the organization's service, product, efficiency, profitability, customer satisfaction, meeting the purpose for which the organization exists. Using the Five

Whys is built on the desire to lead up, to commit to making the organization better, to use the problem as a gateway to a better future condition.

For collective efficacy to be effective, no blaming or finger-pointing is allowed! Like brainstorming, individual perceptions are needed to identify the problem. The problem must be addressed, not the symptoms of the problem. Consensus needs to be reached about what the problem actually is. When collective intelligence reveals the root cause, the group can visualize the end goal. When the team is on the same page, conditions can be created to produce in the future what is lacking in the present. Problems become gateways to possibilities!

The takeaway for the leader is to ensure time to think, reflect, question, make suggestions. Shared understanding is a component of group efficacy. It takes time to reach a consensus. Taking the time produces desired results from the energizing effect of knowing what to do. When the group works to reach a common understanding, they will have a common belief that they can work together to deal with the issue. Realizing that they will work together will produce individual effort and improve the team's performance.

While not considered a root cause analysis, the Collaborative Way®[12] offers additional practices of collective efficacy leading up to the goal of the collaborative work. Leading up from problem to possibility means individual and group responsibility for working in the present as though in a future in which the vision, mission, and purpose of the organization are accomplished. The practices include generous listening, straight speaking, being for others, honoring commitments, acknowledging, and appreciating.

The Collaborative Way advertises itself as a way of working together that harnesses the collective intelligence, imagination, and spirit of a workforce. The practice of the Collaborative Way provides a strategic advantage when available resources are in service to respect, acknowledgment, and appreciation of individual and group contributions.

Group efficacy contributes to leading up, to organizational development and transformation. Such efficacy does not exist without underlying conditions. Efficacious members believe they can make a difference. That belief requires engagement and investment.

LEADING UP

Taking responsibility the Collaborative Way, the Five Whys way, and the way of leading up from problem to possibility means recognizing the elliptical nature of the organization. Understanding the ellipse as a metaphor of the organization reveals the necessary integration of the goals of the organization and the goals of the individual for the success of the organization.

The ellipse is a geometric figure that looks like an oval, a somewhat flat-tened circle. The ellipse has two focal points instead of one like the circle has. Like the circle, the ellipse can be drawn with a pencil and a piece of string. For the ellipse, the string has to be anchored in two places rather than at one place like the center for drawing a circle (see figure 3.1).

When the string is pulled taut by the pencil and rotated, the figure that is drawn is an ellipse. The drawn figure, the ellipse, represents the organiza-tion. The value of the ellipse to the organization lies in the two focal points. One focal point represents the goals of the organization, the other focal point represents the goals of the individual. The organization, the ellipse, is a set of points, each of which is equal to the sum of the distance from the two points. In other words, the ellipse needs both focal points. So too, the organization needs focal points of individual and organizational goals to exist.

The Circle Way[13] promotes a leader in every chair. Circle Way advertises itself as a way of being in the world with a structure for deep conversation and wise outcomes. While not overtly promoting group efficacy, the outcomes of Circle Way rest on the work of the group. The group must believe itself capable of dealing with the issue they have identified.

Circle Way has three points of group leadership: the host who invites the group to the meeting, the guardian who helps the team stay centered, and the scribe who preserves the group's insights, decisions, and actions. The scribe's work is important to group efficacy because individuals are more likely to support the group's initiatives because they helped shape the initiatives. They have influenced the conversation. Talking together, thinking together, decid-ing together produces cohesiveness and efficiency. Informal group leadership promotes, encourages, sustains collective efficacy and leading up!

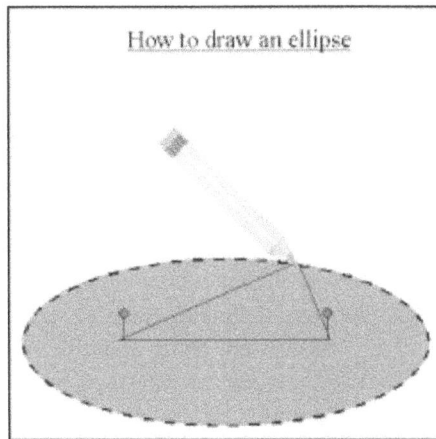

Figure 3.1 Drawing an Ellipse.

Circle Way initiatives have considered possibilities beyond problems of cultural disparities of indigenous people of New Zealand, White Supremacy in local areas, needed positive change among prison residents including positive behavior of those on probation, and re-building lives after exoneration.

Other Circle Way initiatives have included support of veterans, enacting racial justice, teaching how to use energy in the home and business to support the environment, creating community among elder center residents, and providing support for persons in hospice, and their families, as they move toward death.

CONDITIONS OF EFFICACY

For the efficacy of the organization—its effectiveness and success—collective efficacy must also exist. Individuals in the organization must also be effective and successful. Members of the organization must be engaged, motivated, and committed to leading up—helping the organization move from problem to possibility. What kind of leadership facilitates collective efficacy that encourages individuals to accept and commit to leading up? What are the responsibilities of a leader that makes leading up desirable? What dispositions are necessary for someone in a decision-making position?

THE PITY OF POSITION

The lesson for leadership is clear. The day of the lone ranger, great man (*sic*) approach to leadership is over. Collective action and distributed leadership need to be employed to respect, acknowledge, appreciate, and seek the perceptions of those affected by the problem. Problem-solving decisions must include the perceptions and experiences of those affected by the decisions. Those who hold positions that are considered leadership positions need to think about the consequences of acting as though the position alone is sufficient for decision-making and problem-solving.

Someone who holds a bureaucratic position but who goes it alone, or who does the work to impress superiors, is in a pitiable position. That person is a placeholder in a bureaucracy, a pull-up placed in the position by a higher-up placeholder for reasons that may include disdain for those who do the work of the organization, liking the pull-up, being able to control the pull-up, the higher-up placeholder can also harass the pull-up with no consequences.

What is given attention, what is noticed, what is acted on is a function of the disposition of the pull-up. Such a disposition relates to Weberian bureaucratic behavior. Even though Weber viewed bureaucracy as valuable to the efficiency of the organization,[14] some of the rigidity of Weber's management theory is alive and well in the bureaucratic placeholder!

Weber believed that the bureaucracy served the organization by increasing its efficiency. Weber's concepts, enacted in larger companies, meant all were treated equally, work responsibilities were congruent with expertise. The hierarchy supported workers with clear communication and management suited to the work. Promotions were based on qualification and achievement. Instead of Weber's ideal, for the bureaucratic placeholder, obtaining a hierarchical position may be based on personal connections such as being a friend or relative of someone with "pull" or being owed a political or financial favor. Merit for job performance is not necessary for advancement.

Peek[15] summarized Weber's concepts of bureaucracy. For Weber, division of labor referred to using team members' expertise and competencies to contribute to the work of the organization. That is all that was permitted. Overstepping or presenting a new idea was not welcome. Management structure would be organized in layers based on the level of authority. Only those in the hierarchy made decisions. Lines of communication, delegation, and division of responsibilities would come from those at the top of the hierarchy and were to be observed. Advancement in the organization was based on skill and competence, nothing else.

Requirements of the job were clearly outlined, so employees always knew what was expected of them. Rules and uniformity were required and enforced by managers or directors. The work environment was to be impersonal; relationships were to be work-related only. The goal was to avoid favoritism or outside influence.

Bureaucratic placeholders reflect these aspects of Weber's management theory. As a result, the pity of positions held by those without leadership skill or talent or desire rests on the limitations placed on position holders. Their decisions are pre-ordained. That is, either they wait for their superiors to tell them what to do, or they need to get approval from their superiors for what they do, or their decisions are limited to yes or no.

To say yes to a request from a subordinate means agreeing with the person who asks for a decision. If the person who asks is a superior, the answer is yes; if the person is a favorite of the placeholder, the answer is also yes. However, if the person who asks for a decision is not a superior, or is not liked by the placeholder, the answer has to be no. Why? Because granting a request of someone who does not count, whose opinion does not matter means the person making the request is right or smart or thoughtful or influential. The answer has to be no, or position does not count—that's the pity of position.

Extrapolating to wider arenas, if change, problem-solving, improvement are done individually or done with the approval of those of like mind, then future good will be limited to personal or in-group ideas. Diversity and equity become terms not realities, concepts not actions. Repeating the same patterns of thought freezes the organization into mental habits and past experiences; nothing new enters the placeholder's mind and therefore cannot disrupt the present. "We are collectively creating results almost no one wants."[16]

So, what kind of leadership recognizes the responsibility of the organization's members at all levels to lead up? They are leaders who collaborate, who work continuously for the improvement of the organization, who examine and acquire knowledge from those affected by the problems of the organization, who design problem-solving strategies with organizational teams, who evaluate and revise constantly.[17] Collective efficacy means that all are committed to the work of the organization, to the meaning of the work, who lead up together by using problems as gateways to possibilities.

LEADING UP—BECAUSE WE DID IT OURSELVES

Making the organization better is everyone's job. That is what Deming meant by Total Quality Management. The commitment to make the organization better must permeate all levels of the organization. Continuous improvement is a focus and a process for solving problems and making improvements on a continual basis.

NOTES

1. Bandura, A. (1986). *Social foundations of thought and action: A social cognitive theory.* Prentice-Hall.

2. Gibson, C., Randel, A., and Earley, C. (2000, March). Understanding group efficacy: An empirical test of multiple assessment methods. *Group and Organization Management, 25*(1), 67–97.

3. Pescosolido, A. (2001, Feb.) Informal leaders and the development of group efficacy. *Small Group Research, 32*(1), 74–94. doi: 10.1177/104649640103200104.

4. Pescosolido, Informal leaders.

5. Higgins, B. R. and Hunt, J. (2016, May). *Collective efficacy: Taking action to improve neighborhoods.* (n.d.). *National Institute of Justice.* https://nij.ojp.gov/topics /articles/collective-efficacy-taking-action-improve-neighborhoods

6. Higgins and Hunt, *Collective efficacy.*

7. Hubbard, S. (2016, January 21). *17 unsung heroes of Black Lives Matter.* The Root. https://www.theroot.com/17-unsung-heroes-of-black-lives-matter-1790854017

8. Bandura, *Social foundations.*

9. Bandura, *Social foundations.*

10. Teixeira, P. and Carrracz, E. (2015). Successful behavior change in obesity interventions in adults: A systematic review of self-regulation mediators. https://bmc-medicine.biomedcentral.com/articles/10.1186/s12916-015-0323-6?utm_campaign

=BMCF_TrendMD_2019_BMCMedicine&utm_source=TrendMD&utm_medium
=cpcPsych info

11. *The Noom diet plan: Everything you need to know.* (n.d.). Noom. https://web
.noom.com/blog/2019/06/the-noom-diet-plan-everything-you-need-to-know/?upv=3
&sp=google&utm_source=g&utm_medium=paidsearch&utm_campaign=1355772182
&utm_content=453318178305&utm_term=kwd-299095591416|noom&gid=52400
241257|168501916762&type=branded|intent|e&cid=Cj0KCQjwk4yGBhDQARI
sACGfAevcAY-yS4Vbvu7NbS5Z24izY4KvlfdBNCy-b95xS8ltcqdHRoFzyVc
aAmMiEALw_wcB&pos=&step=pros&lang=en&device=c&gclid=Cj0KCQjwk4yGB
hDQARIsACGfAevcAY-yS4Vbvu7NbS5Z24izY4KvlfdBNCy-b95xS8ltcqdHR
oFzyVcaAmMiEALw_wcB

12. The Collaborative Way. (2021, May 12). The Collaborative Way®. https://
collaborativeway.com/

13. The Circle Way. (n. d.). *The circle way.* https://www.thecircleway.net/the
-circle-way

14. Weber, M. (2015). Bureaucracy. In *Working in America* (pp. 29–34). Routledge.

15. Peek, S. (2018, February 7). *The management theory of Max Weber.* business
.com. https://www.business.com/articles/management-theory-of-max-weber/

16. Leadership Now. (2021, Apr. 18). *The essentials of theory U | Leading blog:
A leadership blog.* (n.d.). Understanding Leadership - LeadershipNow.com. https://
www.leadershipnow.com/leadingblog/2018/04/the_essentials_of_theory_u

17. Jacobs, M. A. and Kushner, R. (2017). *How can you become the boss?: From
personal mastery to organizational transformation.* Rowman & Littlefield.

Chapter 4

Continuous Improvement

A person and an organization must have goals, must take action to achieve those goals, gather evidence of achievement, study and reflect on the evidence, and from that take action again. Thus, they are in a continuous feedback spiral toward continuous improvement.

—W. Edwards Deming

Deming's Total Quality Management (TQM) approach relates to the concept of leading up, in that all members of the system or organization accept responsibility for improving the organization's strategies, processes, and products. Leading up points to the science of improvement. Promoted by the HealthCare Institute[1] to improve quality, safety, and value in health care, improvement scientists collaborate with partners to include necessary components of the improvement process.

The improvement process begins with a collective look at a measurable problem to be improved with a clear description of the intended results. A clear description of the design ensures understanding of how the goal will be reached and helps participants and stakeholders visualize the process. Constant learning based on testing, dealing with unexpected or undesirable results, promotes review and revision. Clarity and communication are key ingredients of the science of improvement and the improvement process.

Improvement science formalizes the improvement process. Improvement science has its origins in manufacturing and relates to creating an organization that becomes more of what it says it is, more of what it intends to be by its vision and mission. The organization's members commit to be the improvement they want their organization to be.[2, 3]

Deming[4] described this commitment to improvement with his philosophy that organizational change begins with individual change, that management must become leadership, and that organizational change and improvement require intrinsic motivation of the members at all levels. Deming's *The New Economics* incorporated the fourteen points of TQM into his theory of management based on individual thought and action that worked to improve the system. Deming's management system was based on his concept of systems theory called profound knowledge.

At its simplest, the concept of profound knowledge is the commitment of the individual to transform the organization—through relationships, by helping others learn, with improved practices and beliefs that move the organization forward—to continuous improvement.[5] The American Society for Quality (ASQ) developed continuous improvement into a knowledge-based global community of quality professionals who promote and advance quality tools, principles, and practices in the workplace and in communities to help people, communities, and organizations achieve excellence through the pursuit of quality.[6]

An organization continually improves with the investment of collective efficacy of all members who believe they can make a difference, solve a problem, work for the betterment of members and stakeholders, and the organization.[7] The pursuit of continual improvement is an art, a process, and a science.

THE SCIENCE OF IMPROVEMENT

Improvement science explores the relation of research to quality improvement. In essence, Improvement Science uses research methods to understand factors that contribute to quality improvement.[8] Continuous inquiry and learning are tools to solve problems. Using those tools effectively results in useful feedback to make system-wide improvement.[9]

A core principle of Improvement Science relates the performance of the system with its design and operation coupled with individuals' efforts within the system. This concept echoes Deming's 85/15 rule that 85 percent of an organization's problems lie within the system and are management's responsibility while 15 percent are from the workers or user-errors or human errors. Deming believed that human errors could be due to the system, combined with lack of skill, knowledge, experience, carelessness, willful sabotage. Deming believed all these could be prevented by designing an effective system.[10]

Improvement Science is about just that—finding out how the system works to improve the workings of that system. The process of improving the quality of the system requires constant learning, questioning, and taking action toward organizational effectiveness. This form of action is research that fulfills a necessary component of Improvement Science—providing evidence for the practices and changes that need to be implemented.

Improvement science helps organizations build a shared understanding about how their systems work, where breakdowns occur, and what actions can be taken to improve the overall performance. One of the primary tools of Improvement Science is Deming's Plan-Do-Study-Act (PDSA) inquiry cycle. This cycle serves as a basic learning tool through which practitioners test changes, document results, and revise their theories to achieve their aims.

Using Improvement Science to address systemic challenges can lead to an organizational culture of continuous learning and improvement. Like Deming's PDSA, the L.E.A.D.E.R.[11] model increases learning that can be used to determine the needed area of improvement, adjust goals, processes, and change strategies on a small scale of action research or on a large scale of systemic improvement.

Applications of Deming's PDSA cycle make business more exacting than science. Babbitt, Norman, and Moen[12] believed that staying in business required knowledge and processes to sustain continuous improvement. And, once the organization started to improve, the PDSA cycle was unending! In fact, Hunt, Hunter, and Levan[13] and Babbitt et al. made the case that the PDSA cycle and the scientific method are similar, that the cycle endures and continues with the stability of the PDSA cycle. The processes of the L.E.A.D.E.R. model engages the organization in a cyclical process as well.

Deming's PDSA cycle has evolved into other types of organizational improvement. Examples include Six Sigma, Lean Manufacturing, ISO 9001, TQM, and Improvement Science applied to education. One of the evolutionary strands of the PDSA cycle took the form of Critical Action Research (CAR)[14] that considers knowledge to be grounded in specific concerns and personalities; that knowledge is shaped by human interests and the participatory nature of action research. It is the notion that human interests and personalities play a part in acquiring meaning and creating knowledge that Carson describes as CAR.

CRITICAL ACTION RESEARCH

Based on Carson's learning as a participant in a group action-reflection process for increasing peace, the outcome of CAR actually developed into increased attention and the ability to listen better to those involved in professional practice. Individual interpretation of how to increase peace was as important as the improvement itself: improving practice also meant improving lives lived together—professionally and socially.

The underlying theory of action, the action taken, the reflection on the outcomes, and the difficulties of the action were not to replace possibilities with problems. Instead, the action research bridged the gap between autocratic, bureaucratic, position-based decisions and collective action and collaborative behavior.[15] Ongoing learning from engagement in action research may develop awareness in participants that their own thought processes and mental models may restrict the possibilities that problems provide.

The individual commitment needed to make organizational life better reflects Deming's theory of profound knowledge, the tenets of CAR, the L.E.A.D.E.R. model, and leading up! Action research as a means to improve a situation balances art, science, and process in human research.

The science aspect of improvement begins with an important first step— determining what needs to be improved! Understanding exactly what the problem is can be complex if the perceptions differ from individuals' interpretation and understanding of what the problem actually is. The process of problem-solving needs to include the understanding that a solution may not match the problem. The logical progression required of problem-solving includes assessing the solution against what was attempted. If the problem persists, it may be necessary to reconfigure the problem based on what has been learned, and may necessitate reviewing, revising, and starting over!

What are the possibilities that make starting over worthwhile? If a worthwhile goal is raising awareness of the community of practice to "how their own accepted structures and obstacles restrict possibilities," then what else can be done to accomplish the goal?[16] Theory U suggests positioning efforts in the end goal rather than in the problem and its causes. Developed by Otto Scharmer,[17] Theory U suggests that continuous improvement efforts take place in the presence of the end goal—Scharmer called it "presencing."

THEORY U

Based on Scharmer's theory of presencing, focusing on the end goal can lessen the influence of specific concerns of the organization's personalities that could shut out possibilities by focusing on the problem, its causes, its solutions, the problems caused by the solutions! However, if the community of practice chose to function as though the future were present, their work would be led from a desired future goal. Scharmer believed that the future goal was to be discovered in searching for solutions beyond personalities and specific concerns.

The future goal becomes the unifying factor for the community of practice. The community's action is released from the behaviors of the past that produced the problem in the first place and focuses on the possibilities inherent in reaching the future goal. Victimhood becomes optional, the will to act is based on a future good to act on, to act for, and to act toward. This position of leading from the future has found purchase in other work.

Scharmer's concern is that we are collectively creating results that nobody wants. The antidote for creating unwanted, unnecessary, and ineffective results is the adoption of presencing by the community of practice. Doing so requires leading self to deeper self-knowledge and a deepened capacity for listening, observing, and dialoguing.

HOW TO MAKE IT HAPPEN: LEADERSHIP FOR CONTINUOUS IMPROVEMENT

Deeper self-knowledge, profound knowledge, the knowledge derived from presencing requires a culture of continuous improvement, requires ongoing—continuous—effort to improve programs, processes, systems, personnel. The effort must be to improve the programs, processes, systems, personnel to the point they might reach when the future goal is realized. Vigilance and attention to the needs of those who are served by the organization and to those who serve the organization require focus and intention for the mission, the future.

Similar to collective intelligence, a continuous improvement network must take into consideration the perceptions of those affected by the solutions as well as by the problems. The will to act is accompanied by the will to learn and by the disposition that problems cannot be solved with the same level of thinking that created them (attributed to Einstein, 1946). What level of thinking, then, is required?

If Theory U replaces a rear-view mirror approach to problem-solving with a forward-facing view outward, then there are lessons to be learned. Scharmer recommended looking to an emerging future to learn from that future by choosing an upward trajectory toward what-can-be rather than returning to what-was. Reminiscent of Covey's caveat that people see the world, not as the world is, but as the see-er is, Scharmer's advice is to pay attention to a blind spot that focuses attention and intention on issues that arose in the past—the problem, its causes, its effects.

Needed instead is attention and intention that focuses on the future goal. The leader must be present to the future as it emerges. It is insufficient to learn from past experiences alone because responding with what we have already learned is not enough.

Instead, a change of mind is required—all change begins with a change of mind. Instead of viewing problems by looking back, problems can be viewed as the gateway to future possibilities and potential. Scharmer says the connection to the future is essential to replace being victims of past difficulties. Needed instead is the intention to create, or at least shape, the future in which to live and thrive, to shape a future that is different from the past. Scharmer makes suggestions for developing and practicing the intention that may help create that future.

Replace *Downloading*—same old, same old, worn-out mental models—with *Seeing*—suspending judgment; staying with it—so that *Sensing*, seeing things from a perspective outside ourselves makes possible *Presencing*—living with future possibilities instead of with unsolved past problems and focusing on why the problem has not yet been solved.

The desired mode of operating is *Crystallizing*—a vision of the future rather than concern for the past—to use for *Prototyping*—designing behavior as though the future goal has been achieved—and *Performing*—acting as though the future goal has been met.

Scharmer prescribes the kind of leadership as the job that helps people see, and see together, possibilities as an alternative to seeing only the problems. Theory U leads from problems to possibilities. What about the concerns evoked by personalities and human interests that focus on the problem, rather than on the possibilities on the other side of the problem? Will continuous improvement be at risk or worse, moribund?

Continuous improvement is a process, not a product. Continuous means ongoing. Related to TQM, the process requires total involvement, systemically and individually. The goal is improved quality of strategies, processes, and products. Recognizing that personalities and individual needs remain, using the ellipse as a metaphor sustains the intention that the goals of the individual and the goals of the organization must be congruent.

Which is more important, the individual or the organization? This question has a long genealogy. In the late 1950s, Whyte's *Organization Man* dealt with the question of group-think in which some described themselves as company men. It is true that lives are defined and circumscribed by organizations. Organizations surround lives born into a family, go to school, go to work, join clubs, belong to churches and other organizations.

In that belonging, how is corporateness expressed? How are individual differences included in the life of the organization? How can issues that are felt deeply be dealt with? How is one individual supposed to be heard in the large organization? Who does the organization belong to? Who's in charge? Who says what happens?

These are important questions for learning leaders to think about. To ground the purpose of an organization in dignity and connectedness means that the individual cannot be disregarded when there is conflict in the needs of the individual and the needs of the organization.

THE ELLIPSE AS A METAPHOR

The circle can be an apt metaphor for the organization's focal point—its mission, its service, its productivity, and profitably. The center of the circle is its focal point, a center of attention. Every point on the circumference of the circle is at the same distance from the center of the circle. Everything between the center and the circumference radiates from that center. The notion then is of singleness, of one thing necessary. Like a wheel, the center is the hub and the movement occurs because the center supports the spokes that support the rim and is moved forward by them (see chapter 3).

The ellipse, on the other hand, has two focal points, and every point on the ellipse exists in relation to those two focal points. When applied to organizational life, one focal point of the ellipse can be said to represent the individual and the other focal point to represent the organization.

Each individual has goals, purposes, and needs as does the organization. The aims, goals, and needs of the individuals are served by belonging to the organization. The goals, purposes, and needs of the organization are served by the individuals. Individuals align themselves with the organization in the belief that personal or professional goals and needs can be met working within the organization. The hope is that belonging to and working for the goals of the organization help individuals to achieve their goals as well. Every point on the ellipse represents a connection between the individual and the organization.

There are points where the distance from the individual to the ellipse and from the organization to the ellipse seem equal. This might represent the situation where individuals, working at a job they enjoy and are prepared for, can make a contribution from that position to the organization. There are also points on the ellipse where it seems that the distance from the individual to the ellipse is greater than the distance from the organization to the ellipse. This might represent a situation like disability leave or retirement where the individual seems not to be making a contribution to the organization but is receiving something from it.

A point on the ellipse where the distance from the individual seems less than the distance from the organization might represent a situation where the needs of the organization take precedence over the individual in terms of needed resources and talent for staffing, funding, etc.

Individuals who associate themselves with an organization recognize that the mutuality of achieving goals represents the classic theory of transactional leadership. Moving from transactional to transformational leadership[18] requires leaders and followers to help each other advance to higher levels of morale and motivation. The process has the potential to create significant change (transformation) in the life of the organization.

That transformation is facilitated by the commitment to the mission and vision of the organization. The future of the organization is in its vision and mission. Transforming the organization into its mission-made manifest requires continuous improvement and an ongoing willingness to learn, to find out what makes the organization live up to the promise, and purpose of its vision and mission. Finally, the will to act on that learning is the source of motivation.

The will to act logically relies on the will to learn. Internal motivation is a function of the brain. Internal motivation is triggered by pleasure or by the potential for something pleasurable. Similarly, motivation is triggered to reduce or avoid pain, provide pleasure, or anticipated pleasure. The concept that a leader or a teacher or a parent or a boss can improve someone's motivation is a fallacy—a mismeme. Motivation comes from within. It is the brain's response to something presented to it.

That is what a boss or parent or teacher can do about motivation—offer something that the brain perceives as pleasurable or something that reduces or avoids pain. The age-old avoid pain-seek pleasure mechanism at work! Treadway and Zald et al.[19] conducted a study at Vanderbilt University to determine whether the brains of those willing to work hard for rewards had higher dopamine—the happy hormone—levels than those less willing to work hard.

The researchers found that individual differences in the amounts of dopamine in the striatum and prefrontal cortex correlated with a willingness to expend greater effort for larger rewards. However, researchers also found that dopamine in a different part of the brain—the bilateral insula—was negatively correlated with the willingness to work hard for a reward.

The point of these findings for the type of leadership needed to encourage leading up is that position cannot make others do what they are told. Leaders are successful when what they offer initiates internal motivation so that the individual decides to make the effort to improve.

Problem-Solving

Problem-solving is a logical consequence of learning, of finding out. Improvement science offers six principles for making things better—solving problems—in education and health care. The focus on improvement exists in management, social work, behavioral economics, and education. Once again, the important first step is to identify the problem. Relying on Jacobs and Cooper,[20] knowing the problem means knowing for whom the problem is a problem, how the problem is experienced by those for whom it is a problem—are they harmed, are they inconvenienced? Becoming clear about the problem and its consequences means looking into who has the power to solve the problem. And, if the solution lies within reach, why hasn't it been solved?

Ironically, having a problem and learning in what ways it is a problem can lead to continuous improvement. The steps to solving problems require a network of committed partners willing to lead up, so that the organization can become more of what it says it is. That systematic approach represents the *total* of TQM and requires the systems thinking promoted by Peter Senge. The never-ending improvement of the system is—well—systematic.

Systematic Improvement

The system that is the organization is the bundling of its vision and mission, its people, and the issues requiring continuous improvement. The pull of a desired future framed by Scharmer in Theory U can be derived by a network of problem solvers. Carder and Monda[21] explored the leadership role for continuous improvement at the system level. They did so by considering each element of Deming's system of profound knowledge, by asking questions important to profound knowledge leading to organizational improvement, and finally by describing leadership traits and actions that promoted profound knowledge in service to continuous improvement of the system.

What they learned is that the leader in service to the continuous improvement of the organization is primarily mission-centered and mission-driven. That leader is a problem-solver with a will to learn and a will to act, who understands the system and the individuals in the system.

Respect for individuals, acknowledging and respecting responsible self-direction and autonomy encourage leading up and sustain a culture of learning. Respect for individuals, acknowledging and appreciating contributions promote autonomy and leading up. In return, the leader is also propelled to work with and within the organization's groups who are focused on increasing the effectiveness of the organization.

Deming and Carder and Monda cited characteristics of leading toward continuous improvement: A leader is a coach and counsel, not a judge. A leader removes obstacles to joy in work. A leader creates trust. A leader forgives a mistake. If leading up means working to improve the organization, leadership for continuous improvement will require the traits needed for profound knowledge to work for organizational effectiveness.

What does continuous improvement do for an organization? What does a transformed organization look like? Organizational transformation encourages those who lead up to follow Goethe's advice: whatever you can do or dream you can, begin it! Boldness has genius, power, and magic in it!

NOTES

1. IHI. (n.d.). *Science of improvement:* Improving health and health care worldwide. Institute for Healthcare Improvement. https://www.ihi.org/about/Pages/Science ofImprovement.aspx

2. Connor, T. (2020, June 17). System of profound knowledge. *Medium.* https://medium.com/10x-curiosity/system-of-profound-knowledge-ce8cd368ca62

3. Deming, W. E. (n.d.). The Deming system of profound knowledge® (SoPK). The W. Edwards Deming Institute. https://deming.org/explore/sopk/

4. Deming, W. E. (2018). *The new economics for industry, government, education.* MIT press.

5. The Deming Institute. https://deming.org/. Accessed February 2, 2020.

6. ASQ. (n.d.) About ASQ: Excellence through quality. https://asq.org/about-asq

7. Reh, J. R. (2019, November 18). The benefits of continuous improvement in the workplace. https://www.thebalancecareers.com/planning-for-continuous-improvement-in-the-workplace-2275281

8. IHI. (n.d.). Science of improvement: Improving health and health care worldwide. Institute for Healthcare Improvement. https://www.ihi.org/about/Pages/Sci enceofImprovement.aspx

9. IES. (2017, December). *Introduction to improvement science. What is improvement science.* Institute of Education Sciences. https://ies.ed.gov/ncee/edlabs/regions/west/Blogs/Details/2#improvement_science

10. Aston, W. (2012, February). Error elimination. *Quality Progress.* http://207.67.83.164/quality-progress/2012/02/expert-answers.html

11. Jacobs, M. A. and Cooper, B. (2016). *Action research in the classroom: Helping teachers assess and improve their work.* Rowman and Littlefield.

12. Babbitt, T., Norman, C., and Moen, R. (2016). Cliff Norman and Ron Moen of Associates in Process Improvement (API)–The PDSA Cycle. "Business Is More Exacting Than Science."

13. Hunt, P., Hunter, S. B., and Levan, D. (2017). Continuous quality improvement in substance abuse treatment facilities: How much does it cost? *Journal of Substance Abuse Treatment, 77,* 133–140.

14. Carson, T. (Summer, 1990). What kind of knowing is critical action research? *Theory Into Practice, 3*(2). https://www.tandfonline.com/doi/abs/10.1080/004058 49009543450

15. Kang, M. J., and Glassman, M. (2010). Moral action as social capital, moral thought as cultural capital. *Journal of Moral Education, 39,* 21–36.

16. Glassman, M., Erdem, G., and Bartholomew, M. (2012). Action research and its history as an adult education movement for social change. *Adult Education Quarterly, 63*(3), 272–288.

17. Scharmer, O. C. (2018). *Essentials of Theory U: Core principles and applications.* Berrett-Koehler.

18. Burns, J. M. (1978). *Leadership.* New York: Harper & Row.

19. Treadway, Zald, et al. (2012, May). Dopaminergic mechanisms of individual differences in human effort-based decision-making. *Journal of Neuroscience. 32*(18), 6170–6176. doi: 10.1523/JNEUROSCI.6459-11.2012, 1670.

20. Jacobs and Cooper, *Action research in the classroom.*

21. Carder, B. and Monda, M. (2013). *Deming's profound knowledge and leadership: We are still not "Out of the Crisis."* ASQ Human Development and Leadership Division. https://cha.com/wp-content/uploads/2019/08/Deming-Profound-Knowledge.pdf

Chapter 5

Organizational Transformation

The purpose of life is not to be happy. It is to be useful, to be honorable, to be compassionate, to have it make some difference that you have lived and lived well.

—Ralph Waldo Emerson

A caterpillar transforms into a butterfly, a tadpole into a frog. A pile of bricks transforms into a wall. Transformer toys rearrange from one character to another. Tangrams transform from geometric shapes into boats, birds, and works of art. Origami transforms two-dimensional sheets of paper into three-dimensional works of art.

The point is that transformation does not require starting from nothing, getting all new parts or equipment or people or CEOs. Transformation takes what is there and uses it to, well, transform itself. Organizational transformation in this work refers to becoming more so, more like the vision the organization has of itself. Transformation is probably not a radical change, but an evolving one. Dr. Covey revealed a transformation of annoyance into understanding in the story of the bus passenger surrounded by rowdy children. The children's father apologized for them and told the passenger that their mother just died. The mental disposition was transformed into one of empathy.

The work of continuous improvement has an end goal of organizational transformation. Individual dispositions oriented toward continuously improving the organization are also focused on the vision the organization has of itself. Group activity is likewise guided by the vision. The organization becomes transformed into its vision on a continuing basis.

The culture of the organization is transformed because the dispositions and behaviors and communication of the members have transformed from *me to we*, from members or staff or employees into an organizational community that is vision-centered and mission-driven. The construct of organizational community was studied by Baum and Singh[1] who invited comments by and findings of other researchers about the communities that make up organizations.

Researchers found that the size of the organization's community made a difference. Size included staff, workers, employees, management, technicians, and so on. External factors had an effect as well—governmental constraints, the economy, the practicality of the product.

Understanding community within organizations required a common understanding of the community. Dictionary.com defines community as a feeling of fellowship with others, the result of sharing common attitudes, interests, and goals. Community in organizations can be extrapolated from the definition. The work of the organization done with others requires sharing attitudes and interests, sharing a commonly held sense of purpose to meet the commonly held goals.

Workers, staff, employees, management, technicians, and so on become an organizational community in relationship with each other. Those relationships contribute to the organizational community in the alignment of human resources, tasks, and abilities with the mission, vision, values, strategies of the organization. Organizational development results from members engaged to improve the effectiveness of the organization, to meet increased demands of current and future requirements.

Evolving organizational development into organizational transformation replaces attention to components of the organization, strategies to remain competitive with a process rather than a strategy, to continually improve the organization's effectiveness and performance. Achieving organizational transformation engages the staff, workers, employees, technicians, managers, and so on, in every aspect of the organization to sustain continual improvement.

Burns[2] called for leaders and followers to help each other advance to higher levels of morale and motivation. Deming called for *total* quality management that included all members of the organization who had to be committed to the continuous improvement of the organization. Individuals in the organization are building blocks of the organization's transformation.

The paradox is that individual consideration is essential to the organization's function and purpose (remember the ellipse)! All members of the organization must have the opportunity to contribute to organizational thought; they must be kept informed to do so. Their internal motivation must be activated by a compelling vision of their part in the effectiveness of the organization—"I'm not sweeping a floor; I am putting a man on the moon!" "I am not laying bricks; I am building a cathedral!"

Transforming an organization means living in the future possibility of what the organization can be and wants to be. Organizational development is a planned effort undertaken by all in the organization with the intended outcome of increased organizational effectiveness. Planned interventions in the organization's processes use knowledge and practice from behavioral and improvement science.[3]

An organization is continuously transformed as it increases its congruence and faithfulness to its vision and mission.[4] Organizational transformation is a collective process, one that requires commitment at all levels of the organization, that requires leading up, that requires individuals to believe that their work, at whatever level of the organization their work takes place, is essential to meeting the goals of the organization, to contribute to the ongoing improvement of the organization, to make its vision and mission visible in their work.

An organization has life because its members want it to live. Having a life while employed requires engagement in the life of the organization. The life of an organization depends on the participation, not merely the followership of employees.

The importance of employee engagement and participation has been studied by considering the effects of disengagement—high staff turnover, reduced productivity, and reduced efficiency. Disengagement is costly, employees are indifferent to the organization, and waste their time and the organization's effectiveness. The low morale of disengaged employees can be contagious! Customers are seen as interruptions, companies can lose profitability when they ignore the effects of employee disengagement.

ORGANIZATIONAL SCIENCE

Avoiding negative consequences to an organization is the objective of Organizational Science that studies the behavior of the organization's people. The study of the people within the organization surfaces areas of weakness that can be strengthened to realize the future possibilities for the organization. Organizational science promotes continuous improvement of the organization to make it more profitable and of more value to the members and the stakeholders served by the organization.

Organizational science uses quantitative tools, decision models, and techniques to help managers at all levels in the organization improve their problem-solving strategies, describe the workings of the organization, decipher complex interrelationships of the members of the organization. The organization is the unit of measure in such a study. The goal is to provide direction for moving from problems to the possibilities that solutions to the problem may provide.[5]

Organizational science relies on multiple viewpoints, methods, and levels of analysis and includes a variety of emphases: the psychology of industry and organizations, human behavior and human resources, and overall management. Like any organism, organizations integrate parts necessary for the functioning of the organization's life. The purpose of organizational science is to understand the relationships, interrelations, and networking of the people of the organization, how an organization grows and develops, and the necessities for an organization to be effective.

In addition to considering the components of the organization, it is also necessary to study how individuals in an organization design the structures, the processes, the practices, the strategies of the organization. Toolpak. com focuses on the study of organizations by focusing on the people of the organization.

THE STUDY OF ORGANIZATIONS

The value of studying an organization lies in what can be learned about how relations within the organization are shaped, how the organization can and should influence its people, and how an organization can change. That change must work toward intended consequences, toward change by design, rather than by default or by accident. Deming's study of organizations led to Total Quality Management and the Theory of Profound Knowledge. The goal of studying the organization is to find out whether the members are managed in such a way that the organization's needs are addressed, its goals are reached, and changes made so the organization can survive and thrive.

Burns' advice to leaders for transforming the organization—changing its culture—to improve the effectiveness, efficiency, profitability of the organization began with the leader's work with individual members of the organization. Such leadership connects the follower's sense of identity and sense of self to the mission and the collective identity of the organization; challenges the members of the organization to take ownership of the organization through their work—to lead up!

Further work with individual members of an organization undergoing transformation means providing individuals with personal attention and consideration of their needs, recognizing and acknowledging their contribution to the work of the organization, challenging the member to greater responsible self-direction in service to the organization's mission, vision, and promise.

The leader striving for organizational transformation would do well to observe Covey's Maturity Continuum[6] that describes the path from dependence to independence, and from independence to interdependence. The leader transforming the culture of the organization into one that is the responsibility of each member recognizes the need for interdependence and the steps necessary to make interdependence a reality. Individuals must be encouraged to responsible self-direction.

That independence is a necessary prerequisite to interdependence—the synergy that produces results greater than the combination of individuals' work and contribution. However, leader and worker alike must recognize independence as a step, not an endpoint. Untrammeled independence can lead to results that will make interdependence difficult and even impossible.

Interdependence depends on independent participants. Stephen Covey emphasized growing into interdependence. A basic step is to lead self away from dependence on others, on approval, on external direction, on compliance to responsible self-direction. That growth includes moving from compliance to commitment, to internalization of the reasons for behavioral and organizational processes.

Reaching independence is a prerequisite for interdependence and is a step toward maturity. Independence is also a prerequisite for developing personal or organizational relationships. Individual development contributes to personal transformation and organizational transformation. Transformational leaders encourage and facilitate such maturity so that the organization functions as a whole composed of interrelated parts—its members, its functions, its operations.

The transformational leader has progressed through the journey of leading self, works to lead independent others to lead themselves so that leading with others produces transformed behavior, commitment, interpersonal, and organizational relations. The independent individual, with a commitment to mission and purpose, freely chooses to work with others, interdependently to achieve organizational goals.

The transformational leader recognizes the obligation of the organization to help individuals meet their own goals as well. Conscious of Maslow's hierarchy of needs that depicts growth from personal concerns, to seeking relationships and esteem, to an authentic self who offers creativity and contribution, the transformational leader takes responsibility for an environment conducive to growth.

Mediocrity and indifference are toxic to interdependence. So is leading from position instead of from a mission-driven focus. The ellipse represents the integration of individual and organizational needs and goals needed to function, survive, and thrive. Partnerships, collaboration, learning, and solving problems engage the intellect, skill, and dispositions of mind and heart in a common goal.

Leadership for interdependence that comprises an essential component of organizational transformation is influential and persuasive rather than demanding; it asks, doesn't tell; listens first to elicit perceptions, differences, and aspirations; recognizes and uses the voluntary nature of those who work in the organization; and relies on connections to the past, the present, and especially the future of what could be for the organization and its members.

Uncertainty and confusion are considered challenges rather than stumbling blocks. Problems are gateways to future improvement. Energy is expended on solutions rather than on blaming, excusing, or scapegoating. The transformational leader accepts the existence of leaders throughout the organization and calls on their energy, enthusiasm, skill for improvement. Diversity in thought and culture is a plus to the organization.

Leading organizational transformation requires participation, not followership, interdependent action, not waiting for orders. One mind is insufficient to deal with change and the intricacies of organizational transformation. Interdependent leadership recognizes itself as an organic component that invites inquiry and learning at all levels of the organization. Leadership is viewed as a collective activity.

THE POSSIBILITIES OF ORGANIZATIONAL TRANSFORMATION

Who benefits from organizational transformation? The leader, the stakeholder, the worker, the customer, the organization. The difficulties of organizational dysfunction mentioned earlier—ennui, negative behavior, customer dissatisfaction, the three Rs—Resist, Rebel, Refuse! are ameliorated. There are other benefits, some of which are not immediately obvious or measurable. Bourrilly[7] suggested five important aspects of organizational transformation.

The transformed organization experiences the benefit of a transparent strategy. When all participate in the decision, the leader can make an informed decision that is visible to the participants. Another benefit is uncovering and discovering talent in the organization. A talent search or a headhunter is not needed. Individuals with knowledge of the topic under consideration may help others understand the requirements or strategy or intended outcome.

Working together, being a part of a needed change may feed into employers' inner motivation to be part of something larger. In the process, the organization benefits by having new life breathed into the organization. Workers, staff, technicians, managers, and so on become members of a team working to make something happen of benefit to the individual and the organization.

When members of the organization are on the same page, speak a common language, work for the same goal, a unified, positive, enthusiastic voice can reap the benefit of an external impact. Making the goal visible, providing a clear description of the processes to reach the goal, and sharing small wins on the way to the goal allow clients, customers, and stakeholders to have confidence in the organization.

FROM PROBLEMS TO POSSIBILITIES

Organizational transformation requires vigilance, constant support of individuals and of workgroups. The transformational leader seeks value in change and chooses positive steps to look beyond problems to the possibilities that will benefit the organization and the individuals who are its members.

Transformational leadership is a skill as well as a disposition. As with all skills, there are steps to improve practice and achieve results. The transformational leader recognizes problems, some before they occur, and collaborates with others whose sense of collective efficacy gives them the will to act to make things better. Leading together, they hold the disposition to see problems as gateways to possibilities, not impediments to action. Their goal is the continuous improvement of the organization. Leadership for problem-solving is threaded throughout the organization.

Organizational transformation relies on the belief that all change begins with a change of mind; that connectedness is the goal; that participation—not leadership or followership—is the ethical imperative. It is everyone's responsibility to do good works at work, to surpass yesterday's best as a measure of continuous improvement and organizational transformation. Organizational transformation is a goal worth pursuing, something larger brought into existence by collaborative, interdependent effort. The fundamental human desire to belong to something larger is an intrinsic reward of participating in organizational transformation.

There are steps leader(s) have at their disposal to work for continuous improvement of the organization. They recognize that solving problems is the work of the leader, that collaboration is the mode of problem-solving. There are steps to follow so that problems lead to future possibilities.

The measure of the transformational leader is found in the organization's members. Organizational transformation is built on multiple layers of leadership. Leadership is not just about one person doing everything. It is about everyone leading up. It is about making the collective better than the individuals. And it is about constantly re-creating the team to be better than it was before. Transformational leaders do not try to do everything by themselves for as long as possible. Instead, they work to replace themselves.

WHERE TO FROM HERE?

Now what? What are the steps to continuous improvement, to transforming the organization? How can problems be seen as possibilities? How can organization members engage in leading up? The knowledge, skills, and dispositions for answering the questions have to do with the inquiry process, the will to learn what can be known from diverse perspectives, the will to act on strategies for finding out, and being part of the solution.

NOTES

1. Baum, J. A., and Singh, J. V. (Eds.). (1994). *Evolutionary dynamics of organizations*. Oxford University Press.

2. Burns, J. M. (1978). *Leadership*. New York: Harper & Row.

3. Cummings, T. and Worley, C. (1997). *Organization development and change* (6th ed.). Southwestern College Publishing.

4. Jacobs, S. M. A., and Kushner, S. R. (2017). *How can you become the boss?: From personal mastery to organizational transformation*. Rowman & Littlefield.

5. Organizational development—a toolpack.com guide. (n.d.). Toolpack Consulting: evidence-based, action-oriented consulting. https://www.toolpack.com/a/organizational-development.html

6. Covey, S. R. (2013). *The 7 habits of highly effective people: Powerful lessons in personal change*. Simon and Schuster.

7. Bourrilly, D. (2016, January 11). Five benefits to organizational transformation. https://www.linkedin.com/pulse/five-benefits-organizational-transformation-delphine-bourrilly/

Part II

ACTION RESEARCH IS LEADERSHIP

Eileen Ferrance explains that, typically, action research is undertaken in a school setting. It is a reflective process that allows for inquiry and discussion as components of the "research." Often, action research is a collaborative activity among colleagues searching for solutions to everyday, real problems experienced in schools, or looking for ways to improve instruction and increase student achievement. Rather than dealing with the theoretical, action research allows practitioners to address concerns closest to them, ones over which they can exhibit some influence and make change.[1]

This part of the book will examine action research beyond the confines of schools. The elements of reflective process, collaboration, continuous improvement, and transformation of the organization can happen in any setting that needs to improve and has a corporate desire to make change happen.

This part reviews and explains the six steps of L.E.A.D.E.R.[2] (Jacobs and Cooper, 2016), and describes action research approaches to the steps with references to real-life situations. Chapters 6 to 12 of this part of the book provide examples of real-life research and practices that will help leaders enact continuous improvement of their organizations. While the research in this book is similar to social science research, it is nonetheless unique in that action research requires the leader to be both researcher and beneficiary of the research. Unlike research that studies leaders and their effects, leaders benefit from the effects of action research.

NOTES

1. Ferrance, E. (2014). Northeast and Island Regional Educational Laboratory. *Themes in Education: Action Research.* Providence, RI: Brown University Press, 6.

2. Jacobs, S. M. A. & Cooper, B. S. (2016). *Action research in the classroom: Helping teachers assess and improve their work.* Lanham, MD: Rowman & Littlefield.

Chapter 6

Action Research

Leadership in Action

If your actions inspire others to dream more, learn more, do more and become more, you are a leader.

—*John Quincy Adams*

Action research is either research initiated to solve an immediate problem or a reflective process of progressive problem-solving led by individuals working with others in teams or as part of a "community of practice" to improve the way they address issues and solve problems. Reminiscent of leadership, action research requires collective action by colleagues who believe they can make a needed change. The purpose of the change is the improvement of the organization by dealing with an issue that needs attention. Each time an issue is improved, the organization is transformed to be better than before. Action research is leadership in action.

WHAT IS ACTION RESEARCH?

Action research almost suggests a contradiction. To professional scholars in an undergraduate or graduate program, research is an opportunity to gain knowledge about an area of interest using their own methods without a professor or supervisor walking them through step-by-step. The *Merriam-Webster Dictionary*[1] states this definition for research:

(1) careful or diligent search; (2) studious inquiry or examination especially: investigation or experimentation aimed at the discovery and interpretation of facts, revision of accepted theories or laws in the light of new facts, or practical

application of such new or revised theories or laws; (3) the collecting of information about a particular subject.

Action is missing from the process.

Action research includes two components: it takes action and it creates knowledge or theory about the action taken. Action research is research *in* action, not research *about* action. Coughlan and Brannick[2] described action research as a collective activity with the aim of making something better. They suggested that the action becomes more effective while building up new knowledge. Thus, action research includes a sequence of events and an approach to problem-solving.

A chasm exists between research and practice. As far back as the 1970s, this chasm has been widening.

> There is a crisis in the field of organizational science. The principal symptom of this crisis is that as our research methods and techniques have become more sophisticated, they have also become increasingly less useful for solving the practical problems that members of organizations face.[3]

Practitioners rarely seek researchers or their findings, and researchers seldom consult with practitioners for setting the research question.

HISTORY OF ACTION RESEARCH

In 1944, Kurt Lewin, a social psychologist who fled Nazi Europe, coined the term action research to describe a process researchers could use in communities working to address perverse problems like racism.[4] His approach included community members participating in scientific research using social science methods to solve an on-going problem thus including non-researchers in the research process. Educators quickly embraced this approach and in the 1950s, North American theorists developed and expanded the approach in education as a technical methodology for solving school problems.

By the end of that decade, action research by teachers came under harsh criticisms for lacking the professional standards of scientific research or even social science methods. Hodgkinson's[5] critique suggested, "Perhaps if students and teachers became interested and involved in 'professional' research, there would be soon no need for action research" (p. 142). Reasons for the decline of action research in the field of education included methodological flaws, broad problems, and lack of validity and reliability, teacher workplaces not supporting research, and nationally, a great emphasis on scientific research during an era of a race into space. There was no place for inexperienced or non-researchers.

While action research diminished in the spotlight of education, other theorists in the fields of organizational development and social welfare continued to apply the approach incorporating participation by practitioners. Sakichi Toyoda, the Japanese inventor and founder of Toyota industries, created the Five Whys technique in the 1930s to solve problems. This technique is still used by Toyota today. Toyota follows a "go and see" philosophy. Decision-making within the organization is based on an in-depth understanding of what is actually happening on the shop floor and not on what someone in the boardroom thinks may be happening.[6]

The Five Whys technique is simple and effective. When a problem occurs, one seeks the root cause of the problem by asking Why? five times. A typical problem in the workplace may illustrate this technique.

Paper is jamming in the copy machine. The root cause analysis may unfold as follows:

1. Why does the machine keep jamming?
   Because multiple sheets of paper keep going through the document feed at the same time.
2. Why do multiple sheets of paper keep going through the document feed at the same time?
   The paper is sticking together.
3. Why is the paper sticking together?
   Because there is a lot of humidity in the room.
4. Why is there a lot of humidity in the room?
   Because there is no air conditioning in the copy machine room.
5. Why is the copy machine in a room with no air conditioning?
   It has always been there.

The purpose of the Five Whys is not to place blame. The purpose is to find the root cause of the problem and, as a team, take steps to resolve the problem and not repeat the same mistake again.

Toyota is only one example of an organization that was using a form of action research as early as the 1930s. The Tavistock Institute in coal mining in the UK, collaboration between UK and Norwegian researchers leading to Scandinavian use of action research, extensive work in Sweden on the democratization of the workplace—all focused upon understanding organizations and organizational change in the early development of action research.[7]

With the publication of Schon's *The Reflective Practitioner* in 1983, reflective practice gave new validity to the knowledge teachers use in their daily practice. Schon's ideas solidified the teachers' research movement. Lawrence

Stenhouse's (1975) curriculum work added support to the teacher research movement as he characterized teaching as its own form of research:

> The idea is that of an educational science in which each classroom is a laboratory, each teacher a member of the scientific community. . . . In short, the outstanding characteristic of the extended professional is a capacity for autonomous professional self-development through systematic self-study, through the study of the work of other teachers and through the testing of ideas by classroom research procedures. (pp. 142–143)[8]

The 1970s, 1980s, and 1990s continued to see a recognition of this form of research that involved practitioners and promoted the improved practice. Practitioner-centered action research was recognized for targeting improvement in the classroom, the organization and functioning of the school, and in society at large.[9] Action research spanned organizational change as well as educational improvement.

THE CHALLENGE OF RESEARCH IN ORGANIZATIONS

Research in organizations presents a plethora of unique challenges and opportunities. Van de Ven[10] notes that conducting research in organizational contexts demands that traditional research methods be adapted and adjusted to fit organizational realities. If the scholarship is the creation and dissemination of knowledge about research, teaching, and practice, then consideration should be given to adopting Ernest Boyer's[11] engaged view of "scholarship" as the scholarship of discovery, teaching, practice, and integration. Discovery of new questions and ideas from teaching and practice should nourish and guide organizational research.

Organizations cannot learn fast enough to keep up with changing times. Healthcare is one area that is never stagnant. To meet the changing regulations in healthcare can be a full-time job. In larger clinics and hospitals, physician groups often have a full staff whose sole job is to review new regulations, train required staff to meet those regulations, and anticipate upcoming regulations. Smaller healthcare organizations do not have the luxury of these services.[12]

This same scenario is true for all organizations. Larger organizations often have the financial resources to hire researchers who can conduct needed studies and make reports back to the organization. Organizations with limited resources rely on their own practitioners within the company.

This points to a need for learning communities in all organizations—both large and small. This is especially critical for smaller companies. These learning communities must include the science and the practice of action research.

Van de Ven[13] explains that scholars do three things: (1) confront questions and anomalies arising in organizational practice, (2) conduct research that is designed in appropriate and rigorous ways to examine these questions, and (3) analyze and translate research findings not only to contribute knowledge to a scientific discipline but also to advance organizational practices. Within organizations that establish learning communities, these steps resulting in action research are possible and productive.

Researchers do not have a monopoly on research—teachers do it; scientists do it; consultants and practitioners also do it. However, if they conduct it by themselves it remains contained, but when done collaboratively, new insights, learning, teaching, practice, and theory emerge.

THE RESEARCHER IN ACTION

One essential difference between the more well-known scientific research and the less-scientific approach known as action research is the role of the researcher. In most scientific research, the role of the researcher is theoretically non-existent. Participants in most studies act independently of the researcher. The researcher is an outsider looking in on a phenomenon that may or may not have any connection to the researcher.

Researchers in action-oriented research assume a much different role. Doing action research in an organization requires an internal member to take an explicit research role in addition to the member's normal functional role in the organization. The researcher is a part of the phenomenon under study. The researcher poses the research question based on some problems, challenges, disconnect within the organization that the researcher has experienced as a member of the community. Additionally, the researcher designs and conducts the research to respond to the organizational phenomenon. The researcher has insights for the phenomenon's occurrence and has access to other participants within the organization. Finally, the researcher analyzes and translates the findings of the research to contribute to scientific knowledge, but more importantly to address a need for improvement within the organization of the researcher. One could say that the research is personal for the researcher.

Continuous improvement is ultimately the goal of every organization. Products, processes, and services contribute to the cycle of continuous improvement. This can be in small steps over time, or this can be a breakthrough improvement all at once. More often this is a gradual process and in action research, the researcher is taking the steps as needs arise. The continuous cycle is documented through the process and change is initiated by the researcher who is also involved in the improvement cycle.

But it is not only the researcher who has a critical role in action research. The researcher builds group efficacy as the improvement cycle unfolds. The researcher becomes the facilitator of the change process in conjunction with all those involved in the improvement cycle.

Research has shown that when a task has low uncertainty, a focused intent, and meaning for those involved with the task, team members work interdependently, collectivism is high, and a positive relationship between group efficacy and effectiveness is noted.[14] The group not only sees potential for improvement but experiences the result of high performance. The group believes in its ability to perform and thus performs at a more effective level. This can only happen when the group is a part of the research, led by one of its own. Because group efficacy signals what a group thinks it can do, the level of group efficacy is related to the effort the group expends.

Collaborating and involving the client who is the researcher throughout the whole process allows change to happen for transforming some aspect of the organization. The entire process of action research is action-oriented with the objective of making the change happen successfully. The change process can be seen as the researcher identifies the problem, examines what is known about the problem, acquires new knowledge about the problem, devises a plan of action and executes the plan, and then reflects on the findings to determine the next steps. The process happens from within and by those who are a part of the process.

A GLIMPSE OF RESEARCH IN ACTION

As mentioned previously in this chapter, healthcare consistently is challenged to meet the needs of the time. In most instances of healthcare studies, strong professionals in healthcare have dominated healthcare organizations for years. A hospital in Sweden that had been involved with quality improvement processes for about ten years ventured into new territory when it included patient involvement in two action research studies.[15]

The first study was the neonatal project. Seven healthcare professionals from delivery, maternity, and neonatal wards including nurses, midwives, and nursing assistants, and five parents including two fathers and three mothers were participants. The second study, the diabetes project, focused on care processes for children with diabetes. Four fathers and three mothers of diabetic children and three nurses, a physician, a psychologist, a social worker, and an improvement facilitator were among the seven healthcare professionals. Both studies lasted approximately nine months.

The studies included four phases: capturing, understanding, improving, and follow-up experiences. In the first phase, all participants were interviewed and responded to open-ended questions such as "Can you describe your experiences of the care process, and how you felt in various situations?"[16]

The second phase focused on understanding the experiences from the first phase. All non-healthcare professionals in the study met to highlight common improvement areas from their perspective. Healthcare professionals met for a similar meeting before both groups came together to listen to each other and create a list of improvement areas. During the improving phase, participants from both groups worked in groups or pairs to solve problems using Deming's PDSA Cycle[17]—plan, do, study, act.

About three months after the initiation of the improving stage, the participants met once again to present the completed improvements, make suggestions for continuous improvements, and fill out a questionnaire on the experience. Throughout all stages of the projects, the reflective inquiry was used with questions such as these: What is going on? How do we move forward? What did we learn?

Throughout the project, healthcare professionals and patients increased their understanding of how various situations in the care process could be experienced. Patients reported that they found their roles different and more equal and felt more positively disposed to being part of the improvement team and contributing to better care for sick children.

The action research approach enabled both healthcare professionals and patients to get to know each other better. Initially, the healthcare professionals felt anxious in assuming the improvements for the project. By the final stages of the project professionals expressed that "the role of patients as co-designers was obvious and should always be considered in all healthcare improvement projects."[18]

Patient involvement in healthcare improvement is challenging in many ways. This action research demonstrates how the involvement of professionals and patients contributed to co-designing a model for improvement. While the hospital was the ultimate researcher, both groups were indispensable to determining needed changes and taking steps to make the changes happen. The study shows that

> patient involvement in quality improvements can challenge the traditional roles of professionals and patients by new roles as co-designers. The role as co-designer embraces new perspectives for healthcare professionals that force them to step out of their comfort zone. Accordingly, healthcare professionals are able to view patients as equal partners in improvement work. Reflecting dialogues during the projects offered eye-opening stories for patients and healthcare professionals that enabled them to construct a common picture of care.[19]

This study of a hospital in Sweden could have been conducted in the traditional scientific process with outside researchers studying how to improve patient care. The same questions for the interviews could have invited anonymous responses. Review of responses from an outsider beyond the study could lead to generated reports with statistical results measuring similar conclusions. But the main difference between these studies as participative action research in contrast to a scientific study would most likely be in the healthcare professionals on whom research was done instead of their participation in the research. Their role in the research netted an entirely different path for continuous improvement.

ACTION RESEARCH AS LEADERSHIP

Since its inception over seventy years ago, action research projects have had multiple approaches, interventions, and studies in education, industry, and various business disciplines. Coghlan and Shani report that action research is found

> in industries such as agriculture, biopharma, business and information, construction, education, energy, fashion design, food, defense, health care, automotive, telecommunication, fish farming, mining, pharmaceutical, and public service. It is found in business functions, which include accounting, e-marketing, e-commerce, e-learning, finance, information systems (IS/IT), lean operation management, management, consulting, customer service, marketing, human resource, research and development (R&D), manufacturing, purchasing, supply chain management, research and development, and sales to improve organizational efficiency. It explores interorganizational dynamics, such as in supply chain management and mergers. It is expressed through the lenses of action learning, action science, appreciative inquiry, collaborative management research, (and) intervention research.[20]

They also conclude that action research provides the potential for meeting the challenges faced by multiple organizations today. The potential of action research has barely been tapped.

Action research may become another descriptor for the twenty-first-century leader. The need for innovation in organizations will require leaders to shape creative efforts that result in continuous improvement. This represents a shift from the traditional view of organizational practices in the twentieth century which discouraged employee innovations. This new call for innovation in the twenty-first-century view values innovative thinking as a "potentially powerful influence on organizational performance."[21]

In addition to innovation leadership, collaborative communities of practice will form a bridge between the leader and the employees. In the past seventy years of the evolution of action research, collaborative communities of inquiry are evident in various shapes and forms.[22] Marvin Weisbord[23] in his classic book *Productive Workplaces* showed the shift through the decades from experts solving organizational challenges and problems to everyone solving organizational problems. Action research as leadership needs to reclaim this unique collaborative research philosophy.

The *Action Research* journal description quotes L. David Brown that "action research offers a greatly-needed forum at a time of growing recognition around the world that engagements between researchers and practitioners are central to generating both new knowledge and innovations in practice relevant to many critical problems."[24] All members contribute to the continuous improvement process in action research.

In a brief review of the recent editions, action research studies touched on issues that impacted many levels of concern: health and healthcare, women and gender for a regenerative world, climate change transformations, environmental sustainability, public housing empowerment, giving a voice to children in poverty, and multiple topics in business and management. The need for leadership in action research is critical to the knowledge and innovations prevalent in the current world situation. Innovation and collaboration will dictate the success of many organizations.

THE L.E.A.D.E.R. FRAMEWORK

Recognizing that all organizations ultimately are on a path to continuous improvement, opportunities and challenges will be a part of this pathway. Vanderkam[25] proposes that years of experience without years of improving are fruitless.

The L.E.A.D.E.R framework is one way to engage in action research through a step-by-step process of problem-solving to continuous improvement. Six steps lead through a sequential process of problem-solving.

This model was first introduced to students and staff of a PK-Grade 8 school as a vehicle to help students solve their own problems. The staff noted that students easily relegated their "problems" to an adult they expected to "fix the problem." These problems included not having a pencil, forgetting homework, not having anything to do on the playground during recess. Teachers recognized that as long as staff members "solved" these problems, students would be content with taking less responsibility for their own development.[26] The teachers collectively used the model to teach

Figure 6.1   L.E.A.D.E.R. Framework.

problem-solving skills that related to real life and everyday problems in school. The steps of the L.E.A.D.E.R. model are graphically presented in figure 6.1.[27]

This easy-to-remember problem-solving format is as effective for individuals who wish to assume personal responsibility as it is for addressing more complex issues. Often pathways to anywhere are scattered with excuses and the main purpose of excuses is to deflect criticism. Making excuses, excuses the need to learn to correct mistakes or address problems that may or may not be apparent. Problems can be seen as pitfalls or possibilities. Seeing a problem is one thing, taking steps to solve the problem is a critical skill for continuous improvement in any organization.

The next six chapters detail each of the six steps in the L.E.A.D.E.R. framework. This framework addresses the steps in conducting action research as it promotes innovation leadership by promoting group efficacy with transformative leadership among all participants on the road to continuous improvement. These chapters detail how action research is leadership.

NOTES

1. Research. (2020). *Merriam-Webster.com*. Retrieved January 27, 2020, from https://www.merriam-webster.com/dictionary/research

2. Coghlan, D. and Brannick, T. (2014). Understanding action research, 3–20. http://213.55.83.214:8181/Education/27492.pdf

3. Susman, G.I. and Evered, R.D. 1978. An assessment of the scientific merits of action research. *Administrative Science Quarterly, 23*, 582–603. http://citeseerx.ist. psu.edu/viewdoc/download?doi=10.1.1.594.570&rep=rep1&type=pdf

4. Lewin, Kurt. (1946). Action research and minority problems. *Journal of Social Issues, 2*(4), 34–46.

5. Hodgkinson, Harold L. (1957). Action research—A critique. *The Journal of Educational Sociology, 31*(4), 137–153.

6. MindTools.com. (2020). 5 Whys: Getting to the Root of a Problem Quickly. [Online]. Available from: https://www.mindtools.com/pages/article/newTMC_5W. htm. Accessed: February 3, 2020.

7. Langley, A. and Tsoukas, H. (Eds.). (2016). *The SAGE handbook of process organization studies*. Sage.

8. Stenhouse, L. (1975). *An introduction to curriculum research and development*. Heinemann.

9. King, J. and Lonnquist, M. (1992). *A review of writing on action research* (1944—Present). Madison, WI: Center on Organization and Restructuring of Schools. (ERIC Document Reproduction Service No. ED 355 664). https://conservancy.umn.e du/bitstream/handle/11299/180177/7800002_1992_A%20Review%20of%20Writing %20on%20Action%20Research_King.pdf?sequence=1

10. Van de Ven, A. H. (2005). *Engaged scholarship: Creating knowledge for science and practice*. Unpublished manuscript. Minneapolis, MN: University of Minnesota.

11. Boyer, E. L. (1997). *Scholarship reconsidered: Priorities of the professoriate*. Jossey-Bass.

12. Heckman, A. (2019*). Keeping up with CMS and changing healthcare regulations in 2019* (White Paper). https://gopractice.kareo.com/article/keeping-cms-and-ch anging-healthcare-regulations-2019-white-paper

13. Van de Ven, *Engaged scholarship*.

14. Gibson, C. (1999). Do they do what they believe they can? Group efficacy and group effectiveness across tasks and cultures. *The Academy of Management Journal, 42*(2), 138–152.

15. Gustavsson, S. M. and Andersson, T. (2019). Patient involvement 2.0: Experience-based co-design supported by action research. *Action Research, 17*(4), 469–491.

16. Gustavsson and Andersson, *Patient involvement*, 476.

17. Deming, E. (1986). *Out of the crisis*. Cambridge: Massachusetts Institute of Technology, Center for Advanced Engineering Study.

18. Gustavsson and Andersson, *Patient involvement*, 484.

19. Gustavsson and Andersson, *Patient involvement*, 469.

20. Shani, R. and Coghlan, D. (2019, June 4). Action research in business and management: A reflective review. *Action Research 19*(2). https://journals.sagepub. com/doi/full/10.1177/1476750

21. Mumford, M. D., Scott, G. M., Gaddis, B., and Strange, J. M. (2002). Leading creative people: Orchestrating expertise and relationships. *The Leadership Quarterly*, 13, 705–750.

22. Shani and Coghlan, *Action research in business*.

23. Weisbord, M. (1977). *Productive workplaces*. Jossey-Bass.

24. https://journals.sagepub.com/description/arj

25. Vanderkam, L. (2010). *168 hours: You have more time than you think*. New York: Penguin Group.

26. Jacobs, S. M. A. and Cooper, B. S. (2016). *Action research in the classroom: Helping teachers assess and improve their work*. Rowman & Littlefield.

27. Jacobs, Cooper, *Action research in the classroom*.

Chapter 7

LOOK at the Problem

Problems are not stop signs, they are guidelines.

—*Robert Schuller*

Organizational leaders need to understand uses, abuses, limits, and possibilities of using research to improve their work. When expectation disconnects with reality, a problem exists. This chapter explains how to identify the REAL problem—its root cause(s), challenges, issues that seem to be "threatening" the organization and disconnecting reality from expectation.

This chapter examines how an organization whose mission is to build houses faces multiple challenges that may be financial, personnel and zoning related. The case illustrates how the problem became a case for a possibility *mindset* for providing housing and not just building more houses.

FROM BUILDING HOUSES TO PROVIDING AFFORDABLE HOUSING

In Westchester County, NY, 9 percent of the population live in poverty. The largest demographic living in poverty is women. The most common group living in poverty is Whites, followed by Hispanics, followed by Blacks.

In October 2018, a housing assessment indicated a need for 82,451 units in Westchester County. Further reports noted 15,264 households were actively seeking affordable housing in Westchester County. Clearly, a need for more houses was evident.

Juan Cortia (pseudonym) was a member of the project team for a subdivision of a larger housing development focused on building affordable and mixed-income housing in proximity to public transportation. As a member of a first-generation immigrant family, Juan recognized the challenges and tribulations of affordable housing. His family was once one of the 15,264 households that actively sought affordable housing. Now was the time to give back to those in need.

Juan began his work experience with a summer internship project that included data input for those applying for housing. He continued his work with the company and took advantage of educational opportunities to build his planning and technical skills in defining problems and seeking alternative solutions. This challenge of housing within an area similar to his own early years of development resonated with his desire to help those most in need.

Juan eagerly presented the Affordable Housing Needs Assessment report to his project team. As with all new project considerations, the team carefully reviewed the pros and cons of the situation, determining the current level of project involvement, and agreed to further investigation of the affordability for proposing mixed-income housing within the county. Juan was elated that this opportunity had great potential for his company as well as for those desiring housing in Westchester County. He could envision the new, affordable homes within the county.

However, upon continued investigation into the possibility of building new homes, it became clear that creating more affordable housing opportunities and services could not be accomplished with one program or one option. The size of households seeking housing, the interest in both rental and ownership opportunities, which areas within the county households were looking for these units, and the importance of access to public transportation contributed to making the decision to build new homes or provide affordable housing.

LOOKING AT THE PROBLEM

Juan soon realized that if the company were to solve the problem, it was not enough to simply assume that their way of operating would work in every situation—including this one. While the parent company espoused the philosophy that building communities of opportunity through affordable housing made the promise of a better life obtainable, they also recognized that the promise of a better life required a more equitable distribution of resources. These resources included meaningful work, local health care, excellent educational opportunities, available public transportation, places of worship, and recreation. Building a house without these resources would not solve the problem. The solution would become the problem.

Businesses, health care, education centers, entertainment, and food services face challenges on a daily basis. Some are spur-of-the-moment challenges— price increases, service availability, weather conditions, COVID-19 threats; some long-term challenges—continued presence within a community, changes in economic stability, rent increases—have different levels of successful resolution. Some have an easy fix, while a number require more strategic planning and doing. The first step in meeting the challenge is determining the problem.

No matter where the problem surfaces, or who has identified the problem, seeking the solution to the problem cannot happen without clearly identifying the problem. Juan was eager to solve the problem before he even knew what the problem was. This jump to the solution approach is not uncommon in any field. Every organization needs enterprise alignment—an ongoing process to keep elements of the organization aligned with the organization's mission, vision, goals, and strategies.

Most businesses recognize the importance of alignment. Organizational strategies, capabilities, resources, and management systems need to be in alignment with the purpose of the company. Focusing on only one of these areas with exclusion or disregard for the other areas results in poor performance or no performance.

Trevor and Varcoe describe an exquisite model of alignment: McDonald's.

Consider McDonald's. What does it take to be able to serve over 1% of the world's population—more than 70 million customers—every day and in virtually every country across the world? Fanatical attention to the design and management of scalable processes, routines, and a working culture by which simple, stand-alone, and standardized products are sold globally at a predictable, and therefore manageable, volume, quality, and cost. Maximizing economies of scale lies at the heart of McDonald's product-centric business model. Efficiency is built into the design of its winning organization in the form of formalized hierarchies of performance accountability, a high division of labor, routinization of specialist tasks, and teamwork at the point of sale. McDonald's has been the market leader in its sector for decades.[1]

In this *Harvard Business Review*, Trevor and Varcoe[2] explain what enterprise alignment looks like. They note that this value chain connects the organization's purpose—the what and why of what it does to the business strategy—what the organization is trying to win at to fulfill its purpose, its organizational capability—what it is good at to win, its resource architecture—what makes the organization good, and the management system—what delivers the winning performance. This chain (see figure 7.1) is only as strong as the weakest link.

Figure 7.1   Effective Alignment Chain.

Before Juan can determine the actual problem, he needs to consider the congruence of the five components of the alignment chain in this scenario. As Trevor and Varcoe already determined, each link in the chain contributes to the strength of the whole. If there is a discrepancy among any of the links, there is likely to be a problem. The question for each component is: What is expected? The reality is what is happening.

QUESTIONS TO CONSIDER ALIGNMENT AND THE PROBLEM

Juan was clear on his purpose: more housing for those in need. But his own purpose was not sufficient to define the purpose of his organization. Nor was his idea sufficient to identify the actual problem that needed to be addressed.

Trevor and Varcoe[3] posed several questions for each link in the alignment chain (see figure 7.2). Responding to these questions helps to identify misalignment in the chain and potential problems.

The purpose of an organization describes what the organization does and why it does it. In Juan's organization, his company focused on building communities of opportunities through affordable housing. While affordable housing fits the bill, would this endeavor result in communities of opportunities? This became a potential area of misalignment.

The business strategy needs to consider what the organization is trying to win at to fulfill its purpose. The business strategy of an organization is not static—it needs to be flexible in responding to future opportunities and threats. This does not mean that the organization responds to every possible opportunity or threat—but the organization considers the possibilities for fulfilling its purpose in new ways. Juan had to consider how this endeavor for building affordable homes would also contribute to establishing communities that considered living needs beyond just affordable housing. This consideration needed high performance in both housing and community.

To be good at a business strategy, the organization must have the capabilities to meet the needs of those it is serving. To commit to a proposed strategy, the organization must have the talent, resources, and enterprise to bring to

Trevor & Varcoe's Alignment Questions	
Purpose	• What is the enduring purpose of your enterprise? • Why would it matter if you went out of business tomorrow, and who would care? • Is your purpose clear enough that your investors, employees, partners, and customers could articulate it?
Business Strategy	• What are your offerings to customers, in the form of products and services, and are they consistent with your purpose? • What's missing? • What do you do or offer that you shouldn't? • Who are your customers, and what are they demanding of the products and services you offer, now and in the future? • Who are your competitors, and what are they capable of offering that you aren't?
Organizational Capability	• What do you need to be really good at to successfully achieve your winning strategy? • What are you capable of organizationally that your rivals are not? • How do you become uniquely capable of fulfilling what markets and customers are demanding of you, now and in the future?
Resource Architecture	What type of people are core to you being superior at the things you need to be good at to win? What type of culture might support collaboration between complementary lines of business, if your business strategy depends upon it? What types of work processes are critical to your ability for inventiveness? What type of structure will enable you to be agile enough to compete for and win fickle customers repeatedly?
Management System	What management practices, systems, and technologies best fit your winning strategy for fulfilling your enterprise's purpose? What are appropriate measures of success, both short and long term? Where is the focus of effort and attention managerially in your enterprise, and is it aligned to how you plan to win?

Figure 7.2   Trevor and Varcoe's Alignment Questions.

completion the envisioned endeavor. Juan had to consider if his organization was able to match the supply with the demand in this situation.

While Juan believed in the purpose and capabilities of his organization, the question became: Were they good enough to respond to the current situation? The resources of an organization include its people, the formal and informal relationships, networks, and working connections that structure the day-to-day interactions, the planned and impromptu work processes and routines, and the values, beliefs, and dispositions that characterize the organization. Were all of these in place to respond to the need for building houses?

And finally, and perhaps most important, were all the management systems in alignment—from information systems to employee performance management? Could each system deliver the winning performance needed to provide housing—note merely build houses—in this situation?

Understanding the alignment of an organization is critical to understanding the scope of a project. The purpose of the organization leads to business strategies that determine the offerings to customers in the forms of products and services. Each organization must fulfill what markets and customers are demanding of the organization in the present and into the future. Having the right people in the needed fields so these people are superior in what they do to bring the organization to its purpose is key to having an aligned organization.

No matter the undertaking, all elements of the project need to be in alignment. The researcher must consider the expectations and reality of the intended project as it aligns with the organization that will undertake the project. As Juan considered what were the expectations set forth by his organization in undertaking any project, he compared them with the reality of the proposed project (see figure 7.3). With a 50/50 alignment, the question remained: Was this housing project a fit for the organization?

CREATING A FOCUSED RESEARCH QUESTION

In action research, as in all research, a clear, focused research question is essential. In action research, Mills suggested that the researcher write a focus statement that begins with "the purpose of this study is to . . ."[4] As Juan thoughtfully considered each link in this situation, the real problem began to surface. His area of focus statement read: *The purpose of this study is to determine how to provide affordable housing opportunities for 15,000 households in Westchester County.*

Once the purpose statement (which is the first step in defining the problem) is created, the next step is to respond to research questions that will guide the action research. The researcher must realize that the answers to these questions will not be found in other research sources, but rather in the critical thinking the researcher brings to the research.

RESPONDING TO RESEARCH QUESTIONS

In thinking about the problem, the researcher determines what it is the researcher wants to know. Various types of questions can emerge, and the researcher will want to be clear on what information is sought. These questions and prompts can help the researcher in formulating the research question:

1. What is the problem? Explain it to someone who might not have seen or experienced the problem.

	Expectation	Reality	Match	Mismatch
Purpose	build affordable and mixed-income housing, along with cultural, health and educational infrastructure	build affordable houses		x
Business Strategy	our clients have big goals and tight budgets— our job is to help balance these, and produce extraordinary projects.	our clients have big goals and tight budgets— our job is to help balance these, and produce extraordinary projects.	x	
Organizational Capability	to create more environmentally, socially and economically resilient communities.	A focus on housing		x
Resource Architecture	to design, build, and operate communities that emit fewer emissions, reduce overall natural resource consumption, and promote healthful living	Build houses; major components of the data analysis: Housing Cost Burden, Housing Conditions and a Projection of Current Housing Need		x
Management System	a disciplined investment approach, innovative green solutions, and social services for residents to drive risk-adjusted returns and build value	Limited resources from governmental agencies	x	

Figure 7.3   Alignment of Corporation and Affordable Housing Project.

2. For whom is the problem a problem?
3. How do these people experience the problem?
4. How are they inconvenienced or harmed by the problem?
5. Who has the power to solve the problem?
6. Why hasn't the problem been solved up to this point?[5]

After responding to these questions, the researcher can formulate his or her own research questions based on the identified problem. This is Juan's narrative response to the questions:

> The problem is that 15,000 households in Westchester County need affordable housing. Many of these households are families with at least one child. Additionally, these households are low wage earners and often rely on public transportation. Because transportation is an additional expense, living within neighborhoods that have grocery stores, schools, health services and churches is preferable. Neighborhoods must be safe for all, especially for children.
>
> Affordable housing is a problem first and foremost for those who need the housing. In this case, 15,000 families needed housing. Additionally, this is a problem for the local area where these families reside. Without affordable housing, shelters become over populated, children have frequent disruption in their education, and homelessness becomes an added burden to families and communities.
>
> While many are impacted by affordable housing issues, those seeking affordable housing experience the greatest impact. Parents who are in need of affordable housing have the added burden of providing for the health and safety of those who are dependent on them. In addition to children who are dependents, additional extended family members such as aging parents and older relatives may also be dependent on the main provider. The main provider often works jobs that provide minimal compensation and retaining employment is a critical concern. Transportation to work, school, shopping facilities is often reliant on public transportation. The housing is not the only problem.
>
> In these situations, it seems that government and social work agencies such as the Housing Partnership Network (HPN), a business collaborative of 100 of the nation's affordable housing and community development nonprofits, have the best chances of providing possible solutions to the affordable housing challenge.

Juan recognized that affordable housing was a more complicated problem than proposing this opportunity to his company. As he responded to the six research questions, it became clearer to Juan that this was not an issue of building affordable housing as was the mission of his organization, but rather providing housing. Building affordable housing was a wicked problem; providing housing was a complex problem that could have possible solutions.

LOOKING AT THE PROBLEM

When Juan started this process, he saw a way to align two aspects of what was really important to him: building affordable housing and providing that housing in an area where he knew the needs of the people. He enjoyed the work he did with his company, and he was eager to give back to a community that supported his own family during their time of need. Responding to the research questions gave him insights into addressing the real problem: how to provide housing. In focusing on Juan's responses to the research questions, his insights directed him to the real problem.

As Juan responded to each of the first four questions, he noted how no question could be answered with just one response. By the time he responded to the fifth question (Who has the power to solve the problem?), he recognized that he was not dealing with just a complex problem, but rather with a wicked problem. Wicked problems are difficult or impossible to solve for as many as four reasons: the knowledge that is incomplete or contradictory, the number of people involved, the large economic burden, and the interconnectedness of this problem with other problems. This problem was beyond his circle of influence (see figure 7.4).

Research Questions	Responses
What is the problem?	15,000 households need affordable housing
For whom is the problem a problem?	• Those needing housing
	• Dependents of those who need housing
	• Local community agencies – hospitals, food banks, schools, landlords, banks, etc.
	• Taxpayers
How do these people experience the problem?	• Those who need housing and their dependents are constantly facing scarcity issues.
	• Local agencies need additional resources to meet ever higher needs of those without housing
	• Taxpayers face increases to meet local needs
How are they inconvenienced or harmed by the problem?	• Facing scarcity issues on a regular basis leads to additional emotional and financial concerns that can result in outstanding health issues.
	• Community agencies and taxpayers are constantly tapped for resources beyond their means and ability
Who has the power to solve the problem?	• Federal, state, and city government agencies
	• Entrepreneurs
	• The top 20 richest billionaires
Why has the problem not been solved up to this point?	Blame, policy, demographics, and market forces

Figure 7.4   Research Questions and Responses.

Responding to the research questions helped Juan realize that although his intentions for addressing affordable housing were good and he worked for an organization that supported this good cause, a misalignment existed between what he wanted to do and what was possible. There were links in the alignment chain for his organization that did not match the affordable housing issue. His organization could not resolve this issue. Juan needed to rethink the problem.

While Juan wanted to save the world by building affordable houses, he did not have the means or ability to solve that problem. He noted that the problem was a misalignment of what his company could do in this situation. He was fixing the problem before he could actually identify the problem.

STEPS TO LOOKING AT COMPLEX PROBLEMS

We are surrounded by complex problems. Complex problems are typically defined as those that include the ability to approach them from multiple, sometimes competing, perspectives and which may have multiple possible solutions. Working with families and communities is very different from solving a math problem, finding a vaccine for a new virus, or designing and building a new bridge.

Complex problems are difficult to define because they most often involve real people and there is seldom one way to address those problems. Different people have differing opinions about the cause, nature, and extent of the problem. Therefore, each complex problem in an organization needs careful consideration to determine the real problem before trying to find a solution.

In considering an issue that is currently challenging an organization, a first step must be defining the problem. In order to define the problem, the researcher needs to consider the expectations that are held by the organization and then compare those expectations with the reality of the situation. In this process, the researcher is looking for any mismatches between the expectation and the reality.

In Juan's scenario, there was a clear mismatch between what his organization did and the building of affordable houses that Juan wanted. Juan had to move from building houses to providing affordable housing. His company could not be the solution for the problem Juan was considering. As Juan revisited his problem of providing affordable housing, he had to consider how he could address that problem.

In revisiting the expectations and reality (figure 7.3), Juan recognized that the major mismatch was between the building of affordable housing and his company's focus on creating communities of opportunities for living in socially, emotionally, environmentally, and economically resilient communities. The whole focus of his approach to providing housing shifted to promoting local businesses in areas that once had housing for low-income families.

To preview how Juan moved forward, look at how he responded to the six research questions from his new perspective (see figure 7.5).

As Juan now looks at the problem, he can state his problem in a question format that will guide him to a solution to this complex problem. With his problem focused, he now can move on to the next step in examining what he already knows about his problem: How can local businesses support affordable housing in established neighborhoods? His guiding questions are as follows:

1. What were the factors that contributed to minority-owned small business survival during a period of business gentrification in neighborhoods with affordable housing?
2. What resources were used by minority-owned small businesses in surviving or thriving during a decade of gentrification?
3. How can these resources be used to promote future business endeavors in bringing affordable housing back to these neighborhoods?

These questions will give him a direction for moving forward to solve his problem.

Research Questions	Responses
What is the problem?	households need affordable housing in areas that have established businesses
For whom is the problem a problem?	• Those needing housing • Dependents of those who need housing
How do these people experience the problem?	• Those who need housing and their dependents are constantly facing scarcity issues.
How are they inconvenienced or harmed by the problem?	• Some housing is available but they need local businesses for employment and services
Who has the power to solve the problem?	• Local businesses
Why has the problem not been solved up to this point?	Gentrification caused a shift in demographic populations thus former neighborhoods have changed the populations that are being serviced

Figure 7.5   Research Questions with Juan's Revised Responses.

NOTES

1. Trevor, J. and Varcoe, B. (2017). How aligned is your organization? *Harvard Business Review, 95*(1), 2–3.

2. Trevor and Varcoe, How aligned is your organization?

3. Trevor and Varcoe, How aligned is your organization?

4. Mills, G. E. (2014). *Action research: A guide for the teacher researcher* (5th ed.). New York: Pearson, 70.

5. Jacobs, M. A. and Cooper, B. S. (2016). *Action research in the classroom: Helping teachers assess and improve their work.* Lanham, MD: Rowman & Littlefield.

Chapter 8

EXAMINING What's Known

*I read, I study, I examine, I listen, I think, and out of all that I try to form
an idea into which I put as much common sense as I can.*
—*Marquis de Lafayette*

This chapter begins with what many leaders know about their practices
and development, and how to improve on them. The organizational leader
is the best on-site researcher who gathers daily data about what works and
what does not work. Additionally, action research leaders understand the
background of their constituents and have a closer insight into the everyday
happenings that are the organization's challenges. With this information at
hand, the organizational researcher examines what seems obvious as a basis
for taking steps to improve and transform the organization.

In this chapter, a college vice president for student affairs is surprised to
discover what he does not know about the undergraduate students who use
Thursday nights to drink and disrupt the neighborhood.

WHAT LEADERS KNOW

Throughout human history, the importance of leadership has been
considered—often from a political or social stance. These considerations
were not usually scientific findings communicated to other scholars, but
rather beliefs of social philosophers, leaders themselves, or observers of
leaders. Chemers[1] in his book *An Integrative Theory of Leadership* describes
leadership as "a process of social influence in which one person is able to

enlist the aid and support of others in the accomplishment of a common task."[2] One can conclude from this definition that leadership is a group activity sparked by a social issue and focused on a task that is common to the whole. While this may sound simplistic, the confluence of intrapersonal factors interacting with interpersonal processes has decided effects on the external environment.

Briefly revisit the different types of problems from chapter 1. The simple problem has a known recipe for solving. A direct relationship exists between cause and effect. This relationship is not only clear, but it is obvious. In the case of the individual (or organization) seeking a bank loan while already having outstanding debt or faltering sales, the obvious denial of the loan comes as no surprise. This is not the kind of problem considered here.

Then there is the complicated problem, sometimes described as a known unknown. The individual or organization does not know the answer but knows how to find the answer. So when the car is running a bit sluggish, the owner recognizes the problem but decides to let Tim, the car mechanic expert, handle this problem. This also is not the problem considered here.

Wicked or chaotic problems are in a category way beyond the scope of consideration here. These are usually crises—as was the experience with COVID-19. While immediate action is usually a step to take (why quarantine and shelter-in-place were mandated), this was the first step to contain the immediate results of the problem, so the problem could be more defined and interim steps could be taken to break down the problem from wicked to more manageable steps as a complex problem. Wicked problems will not be considered to address with action research.

That leaves the reader in the realm of complex problems—the type of problem that requires action to see what happens when an obvious answer is not known and all the forces are not known, and yet some type of action needs to be taken. Most people deal with complex problems where you can only figure out after taking some action why what happened. What happens is often surprising.

J.J. Sutherland,[3] CEO of Scrum. Inc. and author of the book *Scrum: The Art of Doing Twice the Work in Half the Time*, tells the story of the rise in popularity of Twitch, a video live-streaming service. The problem was finding the niche for the company to make a name for itself and ultimately to make money. The company started with an idea to integrate a calendar with Gmail. But then Google created Google Calendar.

The company decided to go into live-streaming. One of the founders decided to stream his entire life 24/7. They built an incredibly fast live-streaming service that many people could use at the same time but no one really wanted to watch that live stream. So the next idea included people live-streaming themselves but that idea and the depletion of their cash flow resulted in scrapping that idea. But they did find many people were watching live streams of people playing video games.

It turned out that many people want to watch top players playing video games. People can actually make money by live-streaming themselves playing games. So Twitch was born and Amazon acquired it in 2014 for $970 million. This was not an obvious success story—except in retrospect—after the company took action.

As with Twitch, leaders know things. They know things because they do things. Bill Arcement,[4] a contributing writer for Business Journals, shared his top ten practices that great leaders do:

1. They teach	6. They inspire with a vision
2. They listen	7. They don't overindulge their egos
3. They challenge themselves	8. They do what matters
4. They don't follow	9. They help employees grow
5. They solve great problems	10. They forgive and forget

Great leaders act and they act because they have to act to address the complex problems that are ever before them. That is the only way they can take the next step in solving complex problems: *Examine What You Know.*

CLIMATE, MANAGEMENT, WORK VALUE, AND EXPECTATIONS—ALL IN THE BUSINESS

Every organization—profit and non-profit—has climate, management, workplace values, and expectations. Businesses, health care, education, social advocacy groups, public service organizations generate a place of being and conditions that contribute to that being. Briefly look at each of these components of an organization to note how they interact within the organization.

Organizational climate is characterized by one of four different categories: (1) people-oriented; (2) rule-oriented; (3) innovation-oriented; and (4) goal-oriented. Organizational culture is sometimes referred to as the personality of the organization. The organizational culture shares assumptions, values, and beliefs that communicate how people behave in the organization and how they do their jobs. The culture creates an atmosphere that is felt by those who are part of the organization. The organizational climate is how the members of the organization experience the culture. If the culture is the personality of the organization, then the climate is the mood. Climate is easier to experience and measure and is easier to change than culture.

Consider how each of these climates may look. Kevin was invited to serve on his community's task force to put into action a plan for re-opening after devastating storms destroyed homes, businesses, parks, and community centers. Kevin's past experiences in volunteering and employment provided insights into how he could contribute to the task force.

Kevin's first experience with a people-oriented climate was his involvement at the food pantry in elementary and high school. He found the people who were a part of this non-profit organization promoted care and concern for each other and for the many people who came through the doors of the food pantry. As an undergraduate student, he had his first experience of a rule-oriented climate when he worked at the school cafeteria under the strictly regulated meal plan that made no exceptions for donations. This was quite a contrast to his early volunteer days in his local food pantry.

Upon graduation, Kevin found his dream job with a company that focused on making every employee's journey within the company a success by welcoming new ideas and methods and helping people with creative ideas succeed. After fourteen years with this company, he understood the culture of an innovation-oriented organization. He was not quite prepared for his experience with this task force that immediately assumed a goal-oriented culture directed toward achieving and refining results to re-opening the community.

Climate does set the mood for the organization and also for how the organization is managed. Management can be described as the people who design an organization's structure and determine how aspects of the organization will interact. Management determines planning, organizing, staffing, leading, controlling, and motivating.

Another contributing factor to the organization is the workplace values that characterize the employees of the organization. Workplace values are guiding principles that determine how the organization works. These principles help the organization make decisions about right and wrong ways to work. Some examples (and possible conflicting examples) of workplace values include accountability, honesty, reliability, focusing on detail, delivering quality, being positive, working as a team, showing tolerance, and respecting policies and rules of the organization and the people who work there. Workplace values set the tone for the culture and identify what is important to the organization.

A final factor impacting the organization is understanding organizational expectations. Expectations tie in closely with workplace values. With each value, there is often a corresponding expectation. If the organization values honesty, there is an expectation that ethical standards will be followed. When teamwork is a workplace value, it is essential that all work in concert to achieve common goals. When the organization genuinely listens to its employees and treats them with respect, it is expected that employees will be given the authority to make decisions and act accordingly.

Before any complex problem can be considered, the researcher may become a leader to resolve the problem, must examine what is known about the climate, management, workplace values, and expectations.

EXAMINING WHAT IS KNOWN

While the organizational leader is the best on-site researcher who gathers daily data about what works and what does not work, the organizational leader may also be the most surprised to find out the nature and cause of the complex problem about which the leader needs to take action. Although Rob was the dean of students, he seemed more surprised than most that the college students were the noisy neighbors and even more surprised by why they were noisy.

Thursday Night: Start of the Weekend

Most people would welcome a three-day weekend with evening extensions of four nights. That may be the case unless you live near a college campus.

Each year as students returned to campus for the fall semester, neighbors in the residential area surrounding the college were less than thrilled to welcome the students back. The residents described the students as loud, noisy, messy, and rude. Loud voices and music would continue until 2:00 or 3:00 in the morning. Soda and beer containers were strewn across lawns and yards.

Recognition that these students were living in a neighborhood that housed families with young children and working adults contradicted the Good Neighbor Policy that students were required to sign each year requiring them to "act in a manner that is safe, civil, and respectful" at all times. The weekend stretched from Thursday night into early Monday morning with unbearable noise levels.

The neighbors took the first steps. They contacted the dean of students and requested intervention. As the weekend fiascos continued, the neighbors started making 311 calls. *311* is a non-emergency phone number that people can call in many cities to find information about services, make complaints, or report problems quickly and easily.

Neighbors sent photos and videos to the dean of what they described as loud and destructive student behavior. They finally gave up and just started calling the police directly. In the end, several neighbors moved because they could not tolerate the noise, the parties, and the disorderly conduct. One neighbor said she wanted to be open to college students being there, but she just wanted the students to understand that other people lived there too.

What Happened to the Good Neighbors (Policy)?

By the time the dean of students received the third letter from another neighbor letting him know that his family would need to relocate because of the disregard for the Good Neighbor Policy, the dean knew he had to act. How bad could things be on the part of the students if this was the third family within a six-month period who would choose to leave their homes because of non-neighborly students? The dean had to take action.

A first step on the part of the dean was to gather information from the students who lived in the official off-campus housing complex in the residential neighborhood. Because the housing complex belonged to the college, determining who the offending students were was an easy task. The Office of Student Life and the dean created a survey for these students indicating their level of agreement with each statement.

Because these students were juniors and seniors, the dean of students assumed that they were students in good standing academically and ethically according to college policies. Because the dean did not actually know many of these 350 students, he requested from the resident assistants any disciplinary reports from the current and past semester. Both sources of information provided insights into the situation.

What the Data Tells

Of the 350 students in the off-campus facility, 127 students responded to the survey (see table 8.1).

Additionally, the resident assistants reported that within the previous and current semester, thirty-five reprimands, eleven warnings, and no suspensions were issued.

The survey results generally revealed that students viewed themselves as good and desirable neighbors as indicated in their response to statements 1, 2, 4, and 6 with at least 73 percent of students strongly agreeing or agreeing with the statement. Statements pertaining to college policies (3, 5, 10, 11, 12) and individuals outside the college (7, 8, and 9) had less favorable responses. What was of particular interest are the statements that pertained to the neighbors and an awareness of the neighbors that had a high number of unsure responses indicating that students were not even aware of the neighbors.

The reports from the resident assistants enumerated twenty-two reprimands and eight warnings issued for violations of quiet time, Sunday

Table 8.1　Survey Results of the Students

Survey Statement	1	2	3	4	5
1. MC* is a good community neighbor	68	52	1	4	2
2. MC is a good steward of the environment and protects natural resources	22	71	5	2	27
3. MC measures the success of culture change initiatives through student surveys	2	18	9	11	87
4. Students have concern for each other	89	10	3	20	5
5. I believe that MC's open-door policy is effective	3	4	14	14	92
6. MC culture promotes students to stay within the organization	65	32	16	5	9
7. People enjoy living near MC	16			10	101
8. MC strives to provide a good environment for students and neighbors	19	28	5	2	66
9. The culture at MC supports a good neighborhood		29	28		70
10. The building I live in is well-maintained		9	68	48	2
11. I have easy access to gathering spaces in my building	2	5	98	9	13
12. I believe MC will use this survey to make improvements	11	46	9	2	59

1—Strongly Agree 2—Agree 3—Disagree 4—Strongly Disagree 5—Not Sure.
My College (pseudonym for the college name).

through Thursday from 11:00 p.m. to 8:00 a.m. and Friday and Saturday from 12:00 p.m. to 8:00 a.m. The policy explained that music, conversation, TV volume, and all other noise should not emanate beyond one's room. The other reprimands and warnings included failures to maintain healthy standards of personal hygiene and/or room cleanliness to the extent that it interfered with the general comfort, safety, or welfare of the residence hall community. The report also cited improper or lack of disposing of refuse in proper waste containers.

From Data to Action

Rob now had data—data that told him about the organizational climate, management, values, and expectations. He considered his own answers to the previously stated six questions for posing the research question (see chapter 7):

1. What is the problem?
2. For whom is the problem a problem?
3. How do these people experience the problem?
4. How are they inconvenienced or harmed by the problem?
5. Who has the power to solve the problem?
6. Why hasn't the problem been solved up to this point?[5]

Before gathering the data, Rob framed his research questions based on these responses.

The problem is the neighbors complaining about the college kids being inconsiderate, noisy, loud, and disrespectful of the property. The problem is a problem for the neighbors because they are having their lives disrupted by these students. They experience late-night parties from Thursday through Sunday and in addition to this disrupting neighbors' sleep, the students also leave trash on lawns and in the streets. The neighbors are inconvenienced by the noise that prevents their families from getting needed sleep and from seeing their properties littered.

Rob took it upon himself to realize the college was being held accountable for allowing these actions to continue. The problem had not been solved in the past because every year a new group of students lived in the off-campus housing and the neighbors still complained about each new group. His research question was: What can be done about the complaints of the neighbors?

Rob's data revealed new insights—not about the neighbors, but about the organization and the students who were a part of that organization. His data provided insights into the organization's climate, management, values, and expectations.

Organizational climate communicates how people behave in the organization. The survey results indicated that students agreed and strongly agreed that the college was a good community neighbor and a good steward of the environment while protecting natural resources. The students believed that there was a concern for each other and this concern resulted in retaining students. Additionally, the data indicated that students had limited or no knowledge about others as is noted by the high number of *Not Sure* responses to the statements about people living near them and their role as good neighbors.

From the reports made by the resident assistants, the reprimands and warnings fell into two categories: violating the quiet time and keeping good order. These reports from the resident assistants correlated with the complaints of the neighbors. Rob was beginning to see a pattern of behavior.

The way these reprimands and warnings were managed seemed to be less effective than anticipated. Despite the number of reports, the issues revolved around the two categories that indicated a disregard for others. With a mere slap on the wrist for these infractions, behaviors were not changing.

Students valued community, stewardship, and concern when it directly impacted themselves. Carrying these values to a higher level of expectation— beyond themselves—to the neighbors needed to reset a tone for organizational culture and more clearly identifying and relating to what was important to the organization.

USING WHAT IS KNOWN TO ADDRESS
A COMPLEX PROBLEM

As stated in several sections of this book, complex problems require actions to see what happens when there are unknowns. Rob was the dean of students. His assumptions about the students were not the reality of what was happening right before him. With frequent complaints from the neighbors, Rob hardly noticed how the actions or lack thereof of the organization impacted the climate of this organization and how this impacted those associated with the organization.

Organizational climate is generally easy to experience and Rob concluded that his experiences with students on campus had to mirror experiences beyond campus. Students were friendly, the campus was orderly, and rarely was he bothered by excessive noise. The responses from the survey gave him new learnings about the students and about the organizational climate, management, values, and expectations.

Rob learned that not only was organizational climate easy to experience, but it is also easy to measure. This simple survey allowed students to non-judgmentally present their insights on what was valued by them. Rob learned more about the students from their *Not Sure* responses than from any strongly agree and strongly disagree responses.

Recognizing that the students had little awareness of their neighbors and how their actions impacted the neighbors gave Rob and his associates the needed information to redesign his research question. This complex problem now was considering a new question: How can we help our students become good neighbors?

Organizational climate is not as hard to change if the designated problem is complex rather than complicated. Complicated problems generally have a knowable answer. Complicated problems often have one or more solutions that can be worked out in advance. They may not always be easy to resolve, but with expert knowledge or assistance, one can conclude with a reasonable level of certainty what might happen in a given situation.

Complex problems on the other hand have a number of interactive parts: people, processes, relationships, interactions, and norms that exist and operate within the organization. The manual has not yet been published to resolve complex problems. Actions are required.

The actions that study the people, processes, relationships, interactions, and norms get to the heart of solving a complex problem. Rob realized that changing behavior would not result from more rules and regulations, but with establishing a culture of neighborliness. If this complex problem was to be solved, the students had to be part of the solution.

Thus, the Good Neighbor Task Force was established. The question posed for the students was *How can My College (MC) be a good neighbor?* Students embraced the challenge and from the beginning adopted the State Farm logo: *Like a good neighbor, MC is here.* Students took the lead in establishing a good neighbor reputation.

This neighborly approach included actions within the off-campus facility and branched out to the surrounding community. Students established a neighbor code of conduct application for any student seeking housing in the off-campus facility. The code of conduct was elevated to a no-tolerance policy of any actions that infringed upon the rights of other students within the facility to include only one warning before dismissal from the off-campus housing facility. Immediate dismissal was implemented for any infraction that negatively impacted the neighborhood.

At the beginning of each new academic year, residents in the off-campus facility hosted a neighborhood block party. This social joined students and neighbors in a getting to know you experience. Three times during the academic year students held a game activity for the children in the neighborhood.

With complex problems, changing the organizational climate is possible. Examining what is known can take time, but it is time that is worth the effort to make change happen. Before actions can happen when there are unknowns, seeking ways to discover what is right before you is a critical step in acting with research. The best researchers who solve complex problems are those who are a part of the problem. Examining what is known is the first step in resolving a complex problem. The possibilities beyond the problem became evident with more knowledge.

NOTES

1. Chemers, M. (2014). *An integrative theory of leadership.* Psychology Press.

2. Chemers, *An integrative theory,* 1.

3. Sutherland, J. J. (2014). *Scrum: The art of doing twice the work in half the time.* Penguin Random House.

4. Arcement, B. (2019). 10 practices of great leaders. *The Business Journals.* Retrieved at https://www.bizjournals.com/bizjournals/how-to/growth-strategies/2019/07/10-practices-of-great-leaders.html

5. Bean, J. C. (2011). *Engaging ideas: The professor's guide to integrating writing, critical thinking, and active learning in the classroom* (2nd ed.). Jossey-Bass.

Chapter 9

ACQUIRING New Knowledge and Methods for Handling the Problems

Everybody is identical in their secret unspoken belief
that way deep down they are different from everyone else.
—*David Foster Wallace*

Based on what the researcher knows about leading the organization, this chapter will examine the key concepts and methods of finding the research of others who dealt with a similar situation. Using Bizup's *BEAM* (*background, exhibit, argument, method*) schema,[1] the practitioner distinguishes different types of resources—*Background, Exhibits, Arguments, Methods*—that contribute to acquiring knowledge from the most frequently accessed source for research: a review of research related to issues similar to the one(s) under consideration that also required action—a Review of the Literature.

This chapter considers an organization that transitioned all of its permanent supportive housing units from a treatment-first model to a housing-first model and was beginning its tenth year with the housing-first model.

What were the factors that determined the agency's transition to a housing-first model? What was the agency's strategic approach and how did the agency deploy it? How did the agency adjust its strategic plan as the model was transitioned?

Organizations often regard their own problems as unique challenges, even though frequently, that is not the case. While the organization has its own story, and the details may be specific to the organization, the issues are generally more commonly experienced than not.

Most leaders recognize that they stand on the shoulders of giants. And even though most leaders initially take the stance that their problem is unique in all the world, once they start talking about their problem with others, a realization dawns that others have had similar problems. Conversations—collective efficacy—are one of the first ways to acquire knowledge about a proposed topic or problem.

Acquiring knowledge is more than searching the library or Internet for answers to proposed questions. The common directive for using primary, secondary, and tertiary sources of research can lead to a scholarly presentation that lacks practicality. If the goal of the research is to present scholarly insights or reactions to the work of other scholars, then action research is not the method. If the researcher is seeking answers to a problem that requires new insights, and if the researcher is invested in the problem, action research is a good pathway.

Over the past several decades, research writing has morphed into pockets of writing that some would argue do not even fit the description of research. Richard Larson[2] went so far as to describe research as a "non-form of writing." Others support the research argument, the I-Search Paper, the research essay, and whatever form research has become after the rise of the German research model from the late nineteenth century that is prevalent in American universities and colleges today.[3]

Action research would probably be among the forms of Larson's "non-form of writing." Dating back to the 1940s, Lewin first coined the term action research to describe this as a philosophy and methodology of research that seeks transformative change through a simultaneous process of reflectively taking action and doing research. The Oxford Dictionaries defines it as "studies done to improve the working methods of people who do a particular job or activity, especially in education."[4] Action research involves the researcher as leader of an active search for an answer or solution to a problem.

The thought of writing a research paper dates back for most students to middle or high-school English classes during which students were required to write an informational "all about it" report. Students wrote reports on their State, photosynthesis, the Brontes, and even occasionally the Pythagorean Theorem. For most students, these reports consisted in finding what many others had written on the topic and reproducing someone else's idea. Whether this was called a research paper, a report, a thesis, seldom was the researcher engaged with the inquiry. Even at the college level, Cohen and Spencer report that, even at the end of the term,

> over half the students never picked up their papers. That pile of uncollected papers was a sure sign of student alienation from their writing. . . . When students were asked about the lack of coherent arguments in their writing, typical responses were: . . . How can I [the novice student] tell you [the expert instructor] anything you don't already know?[5]

Moving from writing reports to action research is a process of transforming uninspired and shackled students to engaged researchers invested in academic inquiry. This transformation requires a mindset change about the purpose and format of the research. The purpose flows directly from the researcher's desire to find answers to a problem. The format requires considering types of sources that have not previously been considered in research writing.

TYPES OF RESEARCH SOURCES

Novice researchers in action research need that changed mindset. Previous experiences with research implied that the purpose of resources was to provide information on a topic and the majority of that information and the paper would come from those sources paraphrased and quoted. And the main audience was the teacher.

But with action research, the majority of the paper is in the writer's own voice making a case for solving a problem. Research sources go beyond sources of information from other researchers. Joseph Bizup[6] addressed this problem with a schema known as *BEAM* to help researchers understand different functions that research sources may have in forms of research, including action research.

Bizup's *BEAM* refers to the actual function of each resource. Unlike identifying primary, secondary, and tertiary sources as the distance from the original author's intent, *BEAM* acknowledges the important role a source can have in considering the argument of the intended research. When a researcher starts from an argument source, the researcher risks producing a paper that restates in slightly altered words what others have already said.[7] Bizup uses four sources as his rhetorical vocabulary for research writing.

The "B" in *BEAM* refers to *background* material that the researcher and the reader assume to be factual, noncontroversial, and can provide context for the study. These background sources are authoritative, and the information is considered common knowledge and therefore often are not cited. Background sources could be historical dates, current statistics, and anecdotes about underage drinking.

"E" stands for *exhibits*. Exhibits can be the actual data, an artifact, or a phenomenon the researcher is considering. Data could examine why certain products have a greater share of profit. An interview from a patient on quality care by nurses may be an artifact. A musician's use of lyrics may provide insights into a healing phenomenon. Exhibits, while sometimes seeming to send an obvious message, may require interpretation of their meaning and significance.

The most commonly used source of research is Beam's "A" is *argument*. Arguments are generally the work of other scholars who studied the same or a similar issue in the action research. While a common source of research, researchers do not always realize that the purpose of these arguments is to engage with the scholar. The engagement can be in agreeing with the scholar, disagreeing with the scholar, or building on the work of the scholar.

Finally, Beam's "M" stands for *method* (or theory) that the study may be following or suggesting. For example, an organization that provides training to other organizations may have adapted the Kirkpatrick Model for analyzing and evaluating the results of training and educational programs. This form of a research source can imply or suggest that the approach supports the decisions made in their training approaches.

Bizup[8] uses different verbs to distinguish each category of research sources. Writers *rely* on background sources, *interpret* or *analyze* exhibits, *engage* arguments, and *imply* or *suggest* methods. Bizup argues that it is far better for researchers to know how to use different sources than it is to identify the category of the source as primary, secondary, or tertiary. Consider how these research categories assisted an organization's research that transitioned its permanent supportive housing units from a treatment first model to a housing first model.

Acquiring Knowledge to Fix the Problem of Homelessness

Kathleen Miles[9] of the *Huffington Post* began her article in this way: "It's cheaper to give homeless men and women a permanent place to live than to leave them on the streets." This caught the eye of Joyce McElrath. For the past five years, Joyce battled the uncertainty as to where her nephew Jason would sleep that night. Jason, an ever-recovering alcoholic and drug user, and a convicted felon who was in and out of the prison system for breaking and entering, petty theft, and a most recent allegation of holding someone against his will. Jason was chronically homeless at the age of thirty-three. Jason was a faithful AA member, participated in non-medical detox and long-term recovery programs, and after eight years of sobriety worked as a counselor in the rehab program that helped get him clean. Until he wasn't, one drink, one injection undid the eight years of "being clean."

Joyce knew the day-to-day struggle Jason endured. She had been there and done that. Now in her thirty-seventh year of sobriety, AA worked for her. Why was this not working for Jason?

For anyone who encountered Jason, he was one of those guys with whom you made an immediate connection. He was personable, had skills in manual labor, and was not afraid of work. Employers quickly recognized his many talents and possibilities, and Jason was often quickly advanced in his employment status. Until he was arrested again, and then he was also let go from the job.

Jason was also the father of Carson—just twelve years old at the time. Because of his run-ins with the law, his time in prison, long gaps of time elapsed in visiting with his young son. While Jason wanted to be a father to Carson, he seemed to lack the discipline to make this happen.

Using *BEAM* to Gather Needed Resources

Joyce began her pursuit to solve this problem of what to do when AA does not work. She had a prime candidate who provided background information—the facts and ideas about Jason as one example of an individual for whom AA was not enough. She knew some of his background—he started smoking at thirteen, drinking at fifteen, and using drugs by sixteen. He left residency with his father just before his fifteenth birthday and moved in with his alcoholic mother and her boyfriend. For Jason, alcohol was much easier to access in his mother's place—although this often resulted in arguments and eventually in police investigations because neighbors would report extremely loud shouting matches.

Jason barely made it to high-school graduation—but he did and immediately went into the workforce. Employment provided a financial means to support his alcohol addiction, but not enough to support his increased drug use. His first arrest occurred when he was eighteen. He robbed the local 7-11, stealing $239.00. The cycle of failure began—rehab, new employment, another arrest—and lasted for the next two years until the night he was found in the street, intoxicated and high. That night the police brought him to a rehab facility where Jason spent the next eight years working through detox and sobriety and finding some form of stability in employment at the rehab center. During this time, he married, and Carson came into his life. Jason reported this as the happiest time of his life.

Eight years of sobriety ended with one night of gathering with old friends—engaging in drinking and "just a small engagement with narcotics"—as Jason described it. The arrest was made, he was terminated at the rehab center job, the divorce process and child custody battles began. Jason was once again in the system and experiencing homelessness until he was eventually released. The cycle continued—serving time, release, new job, relapse, arrest. Would this cycle ever end?

Joyce began her own research for "fixing" Jason. If not AA, what could work for Jason? Having her own success with an AA program made her wonder what was different for Jason. This sent her to an examination of the AA program that was a Godsend for her and a required program for many through a court-ordered program. What Joyce found surprised even her.

Joyce began gathering data on the effects of the well-known twelve-step AA program. Since the program's beginning in 1935, millions have been helped. What she did not know was that 8–10 percent of those in AA were helped, leaving 90–92 percent without a successful solution to their problem. She never realized that the program was will-power driven and that most participants revert to problem drinking. She also did not think about the consequences of a repeated mantra of "Hello, I'm Jason, and I am an alcoholic."[10]

Her research led to other misconceptions about the AA program such as the generally accepted effect of the twelve steps. She learned of the poor implementation of those steps because those responsible for sponsoring a fellow alcoholic lacked training for using the twelve steps.[11] These exhibits led Joyce to seek other insights.

Bizup[12] recommends that if you start with an exhibit, you need to engage with argument sources. Joyce began investigating what others in similar situations did. To begin this process, Bean's[13] questions for defining the problem presented in chapter 7 helped Joyce move in a direction for considering argument sources.

Joyce described the problem as what were alternatives for the AA program. She noted that for Jason who was a regular participant in the program this was not working. She now was convinced that a large number of AA participants needed another avenue. For those who have been in a program such as AA for an extended period of time without the results they were seeking, the constant relapsing must be debilitating and embarrassing.

Jason was not alone—and the effects of his relapse affected not only him. Taxpayers funded the jails, hospitals footed the bills for uninsured patients who would show up in the emergency room for a place to stay and a warm meal while they awaited treatment, shelters were a temporary fix to a longer-lasting problem. Questions remained: Who has the power to solve this problem? Why has it not been solved up to this point?

FINDING AN ARGUMENT SOURCE
IN ACTION RESEARCH

Creswell[14] identifies several reasons for examining the research literature on a stated problem:

- To document how a study adds to the existing literature
- To provide evidence that the study is important
- To build the researcher's skills
- To find models and examples in the literature

Most of these reasons support the researcher but not the practitioner. For those engaged in solving real-life problems, meeting challenges in education, health care, social work, or any other organization, action research provides a focus and reason for examining the literature: to learn new ideas and to identify practices that result in continuous improvement.

Action researchers need argument sources—works of other scholars—that provide insights into the proposed problem. These argument sources engage the researcher in scholarly conversations and findings of those who may have similar or even the same issues. Google Scholar, EBSCO Open Dissertations, and Library, Information Science & Technology Abstracts (LISTA) are just a few of the research databases covering a variety of subjects for students, researchers, and librarians.

Finding studies by other scholars even with access to scholarly databases is difficult. Keyword searches often need adjustment by the researcher. Precise and consistent attempts are necessary because these sources of information are vital and necessary contributions to any study. This review is time-consuming and using an organized approach to review the found studies will profit the researcher.

STEPS IN REVIEWING ARGUMENT SOURCES

Joyce's initial Google Scholar search (see figure 9.1) for alternatives to twelve-step programs resulted in more than 1.5 million studies. With a slight change of her search to *when alcoholics anonymous does not work*, she now had 121,000 results—still far too many—but at least a starting point.

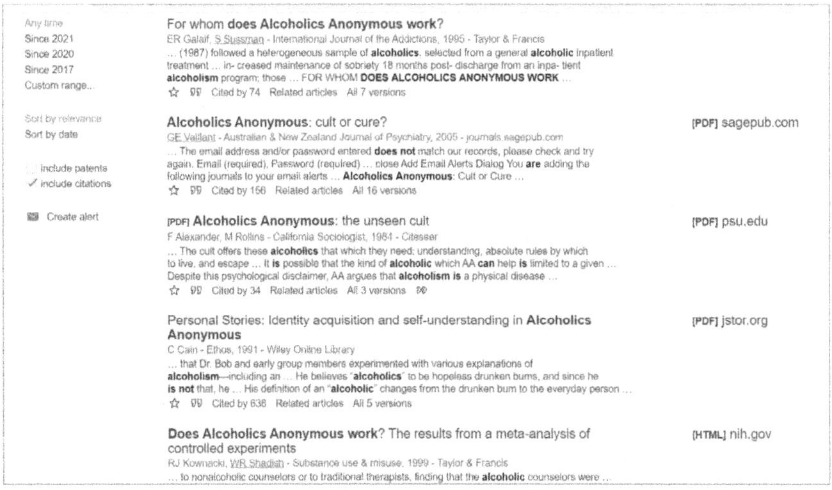

Figure 9.1 Joyce's Initial Google Search.

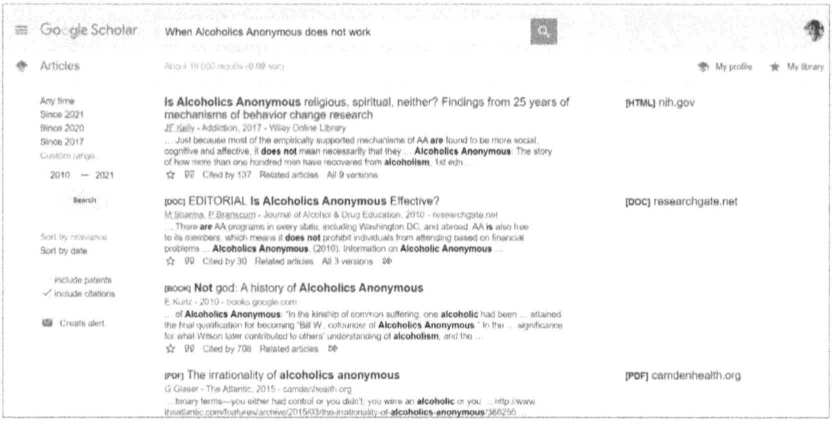

Figure 9.2   Joyce's Refined Google Scholar Search.

Selecting advanced settings for the search can significantly reduce the number of citations. In the waffle at the top left of the Google Search screen, the researcher can set parameters for finding more focused information. In the advanced search option found when clicking the waffle, Joyce set a time parameter for articles written between 2010 and 2021 (see figure 9.2). This further reduced the number of articles to 18,000. In the advanced search, she could also specify her search with selected words, authors, or journals.

Obviously, the researcher will not begin to read all 18,000 articles. A quick review of the article with the screen display or accessing the article to preview the abstract helps the researcher determine if the article is viable for the study.

STEPS IN REVIEWING ARGUMENT SOURCES

A careful and organized review of the studies is necessary—especially when the practitioner has limited time and resources. These steps can facilitate the process.

1. *Read the abstract of an item.* The abstract provides a snapshot of the study in 150–250 words. Creswell states that a good abstract contains these key elements:
   - the research problem
   - the research central question or hypothesis
   - the data-collection procedures
   - the findings or results and the significance of the findings or results[15]

- if the abstract of the item matches or is similar to the problem of the study, select the study and find the full text of the study.

2. *Read the entire study.* While the abstract gives an overview of the study, a quick read of the full study provides detailed information on the participants of the study, the methods used to conduct the study, the findings of the study, and suggested next steps from the study. The reviewer can benefit by using these questions as a guide while reading the study:
   a. What was the problem the researcher addressed in the study?
   b. Why is the problem important?
   c. Who were the participants/subjects in the study?
   d. What procedures/tools were used in the study?
   e. What did the researcher find?
   f. What are the limitations of the study?
   g. What should come next?[16]

3. *Answer these questions for each study found in the search that supports the problem under consideration.* New researchers often ask how many sources of information are needed when doing a study. The answer is always the same: it depends. Read extensively until the information seems to repeat itself. When studies start to replicate themselves or the researchers begin to overlap so that the studies keep referencing each other, the researcher has probably exhausted the pool of studies.

4. *Read carefully critical parts of the study.* Studies are lengthy and technical when written by researchers. While experienced researchers focus on the discourse of the reported study, those new to research want to know what they can learn from the study without having to interpret the research language. For this reason, inexperienced researchers should read these parts of the research report: the introduction, the study section—including participants, settings, and tools and methods used in the study, findings, limitations, and conclusions.

   While all researchers are encouraged to read the whole study, and surely can use data that are presented with percent scores, they can understand and learn from the study without having to interpret the analysis of the data $-z$ scores, one-tailed analysis, and coding of qualitative data. For the purposes of acquiring new knowledge from what other researchers have done, reading and taking notes on these sections of the research report are sufficient.

5. *Write an abstract for the notes recorded from the questions.* Immediately following the recording of the responses to the questions, summarize the notes in a 350-word abstract. This practice forces the inexperienced researcher to synthesize the information just read while the study is still fresh in the researcher's mind. In the process of writing, the researcher clarifies the ideas presented from the study, and a summary enables the

researcher to determine what components of the study contribute to the researcher's study.

This exercise also helps the researcher in determining whether any part of the study is unclear and if critical information is missing. Responses to the questions develop the abstract. Include the complete reference for the article as part of the abstract. Researchers should not include extensive quotes within the abstract as this too often leads to a copy and paste method that can easily lead to plagiarizing in the final report.

Joyce's Question Responses and Abstract

In her literature review search, Joyce found multiple studies on the positive effects of Alcoholics Anonymous and fewer on the less supportive effects. One study by Kelly, Stout, Tonigan, Magill, and Pagano[17] hinted that AA may be insufficient for helping alcoholics with anger issues. Although this study, which was part of a larger study, had several positive results from the AA program, its consideration of why AA may not work interested Joyce.

Joyce's Guide Question Responses

a. *What was the problem the researcher addressed in the study?* The research question guiding this study examined AA attendance and AA involvement to see if these were related to changes in anger levels over time. The study focused on whether levels of anger diminished if participants attended and participated in the AA program.

b. *Why is this problem important?* From the AA literature, anger is identified as a potent and high-risk emotion for relapsing into alcohol use. Anger and situations that contribute to anger—irritability, depression, and boredom—may lead to relapse for an alcoholic. This may imply that alcohol may not be the only contributor to the alcoholic's frequent relapse even after years of sobriety. If these other inhibitors to sobriety can be studied, perhaps addressing these triggers may lead to other considerations of the needs of the alcoholic.

c. *Who were the participants/subjects in the study?* Participants in the study were 1,706 male and female (although more than 75 percent were male): an out-patient sample of 952 and an after-care sample of 774 who were recruited directly following residential treatment. Outpatients were significantly younger, more residentially stable, and less dependent on alcohol than the after-care patients. A majority of the participants met the criteria for alcohol dependence rather than alcohol abuse.

The study followed the participants for fifteen months. Alcohol was the principal drug of misuse; alcohol was used during the three months before study entry; the minimum age was eighteen and the minimum reading level was sixth grade. Anger at treatment intake was found to be substantially higher among this alcohol-dependent sample than it was in the general population.

d. *What tools/procedures were used?* Subjects were randomly assigned to one of three intervention conditions: cognitive-behavioral therapy, motivational enhancement therapy, or twelve-step facilitation. Twelve-step facilitation and cognitive-behavioral therapy consisted of twelve sessions delivered weekly over twelve weeks. Motivational enhancement therapy consisted of four sessions delivered over twelve weeks at Weeks 1, 2, 6, and 12. Participants were reassessed at three, six, nine, twelve, and fifteen months following the end of the delivered treatments.

Alcohol consumption for the previous ninety days was assessed. AA attendance was assessed capturing the number of AA meetings attended at intake and at three, six, nine, twelve, and fifteen months follow-up time points. Anger was assessed using the Spielberger Anger Scale.

e. *What did the researcher find?* Data revealed AA attendance was consistently associated with better outcomes over time. Patients with higher anger levels were more likely to engage with AA. The pattern of results suggested that higher anger was associated with more harmful levels of alcohol use.

AA attendance and AA involvement were consistently unrelated to changes in anger over time. Anger appeared to be a serious and enduring problem among those suffering from alcohol dependence and was consistently related to heavy alcohol consumption.

Results suggested that, although attending AA was related to better outcomes, AA alone may have been generally insufficient to alleviate the alcohol-related suffering and risks specifically associated with anger. Changes in anger were found to be unrelated to the degree of AA attendance.

This contrast to the explicit emphasis in AA literature on reducing anger could be reflecting the reality that, despite the emphatic emphasis in AA core literature on reducing anger, AA attendance itself does not lead directly to reductions in anger. However, it may be that, although the levels of anger remain quite high, AA helps attendees improve their ability to successfully tolerate anger.

f. *What are the limitations of the study?* Measurement, sampling, or the time frame for applying assessment factors may have contributed to the lack of association between AA and anger. The AA literature on reducing anger may be outdated. Different forms of anger (suppression vs.

reactivity, appropriate vs. inappropriate expression) need to be considered to improve moving from holding on to anger to reducing anger.

What should come next? Although absolute levels are not changing in response to AA, attendees may improve in their ability to manage anger. This is an area for continued study. More detailed research regarding the effects of involvement in AA is clearly needed. Results suggested that AA attendance alone may be insufficient to alleviate the suffering and alcohol-related risks specifically associated with anger.

JOYCE'S GUIDE QUESTION RESPONSES

a. *What was the problem the researcher addressed in the study?* The research question guiding this study was: Is anger related to relapse risk and can AA attendance help mitigate that risk? The researchers found that anger is singled out as a high-risk emotion for relapse to alcohol use: "Resentment is the number one offender. It destroys more alcoholics than anything else. . . . If we were to live we had to be free of anger."[18]

b. *Why is the problem important?* With all the other aspects of the program, including the twelve steps and regular AA attendance, if elevated levels of anger continued, the participant was in danger of relapse. Higher levels of anger were associated with heavier drinking.

c. *Who were the participants/subjects in the study?* In this study, there were 1,706 alcohol-dependent men and women. All participants were receiving treatment and were assessed at intake, three, six, nine, twelve, and fifteen months intervals. The participants had substantially elevated levels of anger (98 percent) compared to the general population. Participants were part of an out-patient sample (952) or an after-care sample (774). The after-care samples were recruited directly following residential treatment. Out-patient participants were significantly younger, more residentially stable, and less dependent on alcohol than the after-care patients.

d. *What tools/procedures were used?* After recruitment, participants were randomly assigned to a program: cognitive-behavioral therapy, motivational enhancement therapy, or twelve-step facilitation. The twelve step and cognitive-behavioral therapy consisted of twelve sessions delivered weekly over twelve weeks. The motivational enhancement therapy consisted of four sessions delivered over twelve weeks at Week 1, 2, 6, and 12. Three measures were used: (1) estimates of alcohol consumption, (2) AA attendance, and (3) a 15-item anger scale.

e. *What did the researcher find?* Elevated levels of anger decreased from 98 percentile to 89 percentile but still remained high after the fifteen months in the study. AA attendance was associated with better drinking outcomes and higher levels of anger was associated with heavier drinking. Results suggested that AA attendance alone may not be sufficient to alleviate alcohol-related risks specifically associated with anger.

f. *What are the limitations of the study?* Although not specifically mentioned in this study, the multiple variables in the study—out-patient and after-care sampling, the three different programs, the gathering of data permitted by the program—all contributed to the limited generalizability of the study. The study mentioned that measurement, sampling, or assessment time frame factors may have contributed to the lack of association between AA and anger.

g. *What should come next?* This study suggests that anger appears to be a serious and enduring problem among those suffering from alcohol dependence and is consistently related to heavy alcohol consumption. Addressing issues that relate to anger—including irritability, depression, and boredom—as well as other possible issues including lack of self-efficacy warrant study for individuals for whom AA is not working.[19]

Once Joyce answered the seven guide questions, she used the information to create her own abstract of the study. She included the reference information at the beginning of the abstract so she would have the information to include in her reference section in her study. Joyce's abstract is in figure 9.3.

Joyce acquired new knowledge through the first three parts of the BEAM format. She continued reviewing studies on alcoholics and anger and sought additional studies on independent housing in lieu of detox programs. While this study was in an initial stage, she gained clearer directions for choosing a method or theory (the *M* in BEAM) to devise a plan.

The researcher used the same format to review each study for its support of the researcher's current study: read the study with a focus on the introduction, the components, findings, conclusions, limitations, and recommendations for future studies. While reading, answer the seven guide questions. Next, create an abstract of about 350 words to summarize the study and to consider how the study supports or suggests ideas for developing the new study.

The abstract serves to support ideas for the plan, the method for enacting the ideas, and the underlying theory supporting the plan. These will be examined in the next chapter for devising the plan. New and nearly new researchers may need to justify plans to implement their ideas. The research abstracts can serve this purpose, and the researcher can share the abstract with the administration prior to undertaking the plan as evidence to support the plan.

Kelly, J. F., Stout, R. L., Tonigan, J. S., Magill, M., & Pagano, M. E. (2010). Negative affect, relapse, and Alcoholics Anonymous (AA): does AA work by reducing anger?. *Journal of Studies on Alcohol and Drugs, 71*(3), 434-444.

AA has been a program promoting recovery for alcoholics since the 1930s. The program is international and widely used by participants as a support to overcome alcohol abuse. Numerous studies have examined the relationship between AA attendance and drinking behavior. Fewer studies have examined how AA attendance may facilitate recovery.

In the study by Kelly, Stout, Tonigan, Magill, and Pagano (2010), the researchers examined whether AA participation and attendance impacted 1,706 alcohol dependent adults who had elevated levels of anger were helped by the program. The researchers found that AA attendance alone did not alleviate alcohol related risks specifically associated with anger.

While the study included three different treatment programs over a 15-month period and involved regular support sessions in addition to the AA program, the anger levels of the participants were not mitigated enough to control alcohol intake and prevent alcohol abuse relapse.

The study did find that issues of anger, depression, irritability, and boredom contributed to higher levels of alcohol consumption; that AA was unrelated to anger; that anger partially mediated AA's relationship to sobriety was not supported by the study. The researchers recommended future studies to clarify the exact nature and direction of the relationship that heavy drinking may exacerbate anger. Other related issues that may increase alcohol dependence also needed to be studied.

This one study suggested that AA is not a solution for every alcoholic. Other approaches to assisting alcoholics need consideration when this highly popular program does not work.

Figure 9.3   Joyce's Abstract of Kelly, Stout, Tonigan, Magill, and Pagano.

NOTES

1. Bizup, J. (2008). BEAM: A rhetorical vocabulary for teaching research-based writing. *Rhetoric Review, 27*(1), 72–86.

2. Larson, Richard L. (1982). The research paper in the writing course: A non-form of writing. *College English, 44*(8), 811–816.

3. Bizup, BEAM.

4. Action research. (2020). *Oxford Learners Dictionaries*. Retrieved from https://www.oxfordlearnersdictionaries.com/definition/american_english/action-research

5. Cohen, A. J. and Spencer, J. (1993). Using writing across the curriculum in economics: Is taking the plunge worth it? *Journal of Economic Education, 23*, 219–230.

6. Bizup, BEAM.

7. Bizup, BEAM, 82.

8. Bizup, BEAM.

9. Miles, K. (2014, Mar. 25). Housing the homeless not only saves lives—It's actually cheaper than doing nothing. *Huffington Post*, https://www.huffpost.com/entry/housing-first-homeless-charlotte_n_5022628

10. Beck, C. (2017). *Alcohol lied to me: The intelligent way to escape alcohol addiction*. New York: (n.p.).

11. Breuninger, M. M., Grosso, J. A., Hunter, W., and Dolan, S. L. (2020). Treatment of alcohol use disorder: Integration of Alcoholics Anonymous and cognitive behavioral therapy. *Training and Education in Professional Psychology, 14*(1), 19.

12. Bizup, BEAM.

13. Bean, J. C. (2011). *Engaging ideas: The professor's guide to integrating writing, critical thinking, and active learning in the classroom* (2nd ed.). Jossey-Bass.

14. Creswell, J. W. and Creswell, J. D. (2018) *Research design: Qualitative, quantitative, and mixed methods approaches.* Sage.

15. Creswell and Creswell, *Research design*, 287.

16. Jacobs, M. A. and Cooper, B. S. (2016). *Action research in the classroom: Helping teachers assess and improve their work.* Rowman & Littlefield, 90.

17. Kelly, J. F., Stout, R. L., Tonigan, J. S., Magill, M., and Pagano, M. E. (2010). Negative affect, relapse, and Alcoholics Anonymous (AA): Does AA work by reducing anger? *Journal of Studies on Alcohol and Drugs, 71*(3), 434–444.

18. Alcoholics Anonymous. (2001). *Alcoholics Anonymous: The story of how thousands of men and women have recovered from alcoholism* (4th ed.). Alcoholics Anonymous World Services, 64, 66.

19. Kelly et al., *Negative affect, relapse.*

Chapter 10

DEVISING a Plan

Have a bias toward action—let's see something happen now.
You can break that big plan into small steps and take the first step
right away.

—Indira Gandhi

Each leader needs to devise a plan to carry out the action research. Once the problem/challenge is identified, contributing factors to the problem are recognized, and research from others with similar situations is studied, and a proposed course of action is planned. This chapter will use the experience of a parent of a junior student in high school and that of a teacher of first graders to address the issue of vaping in her local community. The chapter details the steps in creating a plan of action.

PLANNING AS A PART OF LIFE

Planning is a natural part of life. We plan trips, celebrations, and meals. We use road maps, blueprints, and lists. We use plans to get from one place to a desired next place. Even new and nearly new members of an organization have been part of planning. For most individuals in this category, the greatest plan was getting to college and then getting out of college. The idea of planning is quite common.

Successful planning is not quite as common as the planning process. Taking a road trip today involves reliance on the GPS (Global Positioning System). A GPS answers several questions: *Where am I now? Where am I going? When will I get there?* and *What is the best way to get there?* These are basically the same questions a leader researcher needs to ask when planning to make a change and use action research to initiate continuous improvement.

PLANNING: EVERY LEADER'S CALL

Any project worth doing requires planning to make change happen. Dyan Crace's[1] post on TakingPoint Leadership lists seven steps in the form of questions for effective planning:

1. What's our objective?
2. Are there any roadblocks?
3. What resources can we utilize?
4. What have we learned from past planning sessions?
5. What actions do we need to take?
6. How might this plan fail?
7. What are our contingencies?

Crace states that bringing a team together is essential for effective planning. The team needs to be centered on an aligned objective, specific strategy, and goals that define actions for execution. Crace warns that 60 percent of plans fail due to a lack of alignment and accountability.

Of the seven suggested questions, identifying the objective requires all members of the team to agree on what they are trying to accomplish. Objectives need to be concise, timebound, quantifiable, and rooted in the mission of the organization. The response to this question determines how every other question will be answered and determines the effectiveness of the planning.

Four of the questions require a reality check: roadblocks, needed resources, previous planning, and possibilities for failure before the team can consider the actions they need to take. And, as with all effective planning, a contingency plan needs to be considered. More about contingency plans will be developed in chapter 11 (Executing-Evaluating the Plan) and chapter 12 (Repeating the Steps as Needed).

PLANNING IN FULL VIEW

Maureen, a first-grade teacher, became obsessed with an issue that generally has minimal impact on first graders: vaping. But Maureen was a teacher second and a parent first. Maureen's sixteen-year-old son, Jonathan, was a junior in the local high school. Maureen and Jonathan had some conversations on the topic of smoking, but she was quite surprised to hear his take on vaping not being a form of smoking. This was prior to the FDA regulation in December 2019 banning the sale of all tobacco products to anyone under the age of twenty-one.

Jonathan, generally recognized by his mother, teachers, and school personnel as a good kid, was also in the midst of 1,200 peers at the local high school. Jonathan revealed that vaping was a regular activity in the boys' bathroom at school and in the football locker room. He assured his mother that he was not among the vapers but admitted that some of his teammates were vaping.

Maureen, distraught by this revelation, began fretting over the most appropriate course of action. Should she call the principal? Should she contact her son's football coach? While smoking was prohibited in all schools, why was prohibition of vaping not as stringent?

Maureen began her own research on the topic. JUUL Inc. had recently become popular with teens and their sweet flavors (mango and crème brulee) were readily available at gas stations and convenience stores. She noted the products at the convenience store that was in close proximity to the high school. She read that many store owners and gas clerks seldom checked for any age identity, so it was as easy for high-school students to acquire the products as it was to backpack a package of candy.

In continuing her own research, Maureen was dismayed to find that the increase of vaping between 2017 and 2018 was significant (see figure 10.1).

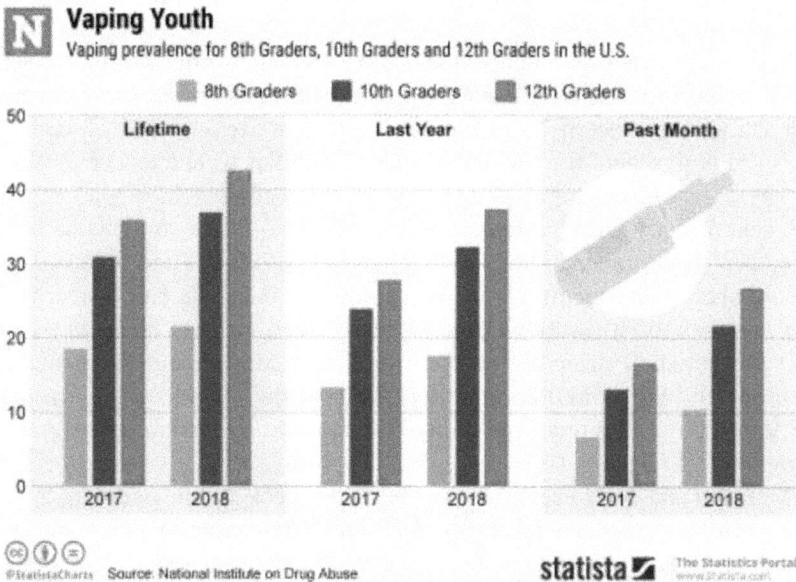

Figure 10.1   Vaping Stats between 2017 and 2018.

When she closely examined this chart, she was even more upset by the report that eighth graders were among the vapers. Could this be true? She worked in a K-8 school. Could this be happening in her school? Wouldn't someone notice?

Maureen could no longer be a quiet bystander on the issue. While spending her planning period in the faculty room, Tony, one of the middle-school teachers, stopped by for a cup of coffee. Maureen asked if he was aware of the vaping situation currently unfolding. Tony admitted having some awareness but was not overly informed on the issue. Maureen showed him the chart and he was as surprised as she was at the prevalence of eighth grade students already vaping. She posed to Tony the question that had been bothering her: Could this be happening in our school?

The most "convenient" spot for vaping in the school would have to be in the bathrooms. Faculty had their own restrooms and had no reason to be in student bathrooms. In fact, faulty were not permitted by law to use student restrooms. So, did anyone supervise the use of the bathrooms? How convenient for students to have a gathering place that was off limits to faculty.

Tony and Maureen decided this needed further investigation in their own school. They made an initial plan to meet with the assistant principal of the middle-school division. They presented the chart as their first form of evidence of concern. They further delineated the concern of unsupervised bathrooms and they also made mention of the availability of vaping products at the convenience store and gas station that were within walking distance of the school.

They had no actual evidence that vaping was happening with the students in or even near the school. Their main objective was awareness of a developing nationwide concern. Maureen also shared that her son knew of vaping at the local high school for which their school families were a feeder.

The assistant principal listened to their concern. While Maureen did not deal directly with the middle-school students, these students had once been her "first graders." She knew many of the families and believed they would share her concern about the vaping. Further, she had concerns for the high-school students who had already been vaping. Maureen, Tony, and the assistant principal agreed that a first step would be in making families and the school community aware of the situation. The assistant principal gave Maureen and Tony full latitude to design an awareness program.

Maureen and Tony sketched some needed aspects of this planning: potential roadblocks, needed resources, learnings from other school initiatives, possible actions, possible failures, and contingency planning. Creating an awareness program seemed the most efficacious route for moving forward because awareness did not accuse or attack but offered information.

Parts of this planning were readily obvious. The potential roadblocks surfaced quickly: denial of the situation at a middle-school level, lack of interest on the part of parents/guardians, cover up by students, lack of funding to support an awareness program, insufficient knowledge on the impact of vaping, teacher support of the awareness initiative.

The roadblocks helped Maureen and Tony realize some resources they would need to make this awareness program viable. The people category had the greatest need as a resource:

(1) parents/guardians needed to show interest and support in the initiative; (2) teachers within the school had to be advocates of awareness; (3) students—particularly the middle-school students—had to receive instruction on the effects of vaping. Beyond the people resources, they would need programs to make this happen and resources within the community to support the initiative.

Maureen and Tony focused on action steps to bring about awareness. They identified three key elements to promote awareness: student awareness through a wellness curriculum; parent awareness through a workshop that featured a prominent doctor, state senator/legislator, local police/community officers; and teacher awareness through a workshop on the curriculum.

They also considered ways this awareness initiative could fail. One strong consideration was parents/guardians regarding vaping as a high-school issue with little impact on middle school. Because of this realization, Maureen and Tony decided to invite the local high school and involve them in this awareness initiative also.

Although they were convinced that joining middle and high school in the initiative would have far greater impact, they also considered a contingency plan if this did not materialize. The concern that the awareness campaign would backfire and make vaping more attractive to middle and high-school students loomed before them as the worst possible scenario. They knew they had to hope for the best and plan for the worst.

A PROPOSAL FOR SUCCESS

In creating an initiative for improvement, following directives from a planned proposal can be very helpful. The purpose of a proposal is to convince readers that the proposed research is worthwhile, and that the researcher has the competence and a viable plan to complete it. A strong and highly developed proposal lays a foundation for successful action research.

Proposals for an action research study should be one to two pages in length. A solid proposal includes the following:

1. *Clear statement of research question*—Very clearly state what you will be studying. Be sure that this is understandable to someone who does not know much about the field of study. If needed, define terms. To test the explanation, give the proposal to a friend not familiar with the planned initiative. If your friend does not understand, try again! Then ask a colleague or professional in the field if this research question is pertinent for the group.
2. *Project goal and objectives*—Goals and objectives are often confused with each other. They both describe things that a person may want to achieve or attain but in relative terms may mean different things. Both are desired outcomes of work done by a person but what sets them apart is the time frame, attributes they are set for, and the effect they have. Both terms reference the target that the effort hopes to accomplish.

Example

• Goal: Prevent the use of vaping among middle and high-school students.
• Objective: An awareness program on vaping will be developed and implemented to provide information to middle and high-school students, parents/guardians, and teachers about the dangers of vaping that affect our teens across the nation. The hope is curtailing the teen vaping epidemic locally.

NOTE: #1 and 2 are important, the most important part of the proposal. The rest of the proposal supports these statements. These two components do not need to be long—one short paragraph should be enough—but this paragraph is the most critical. The rest of the proposal will explain why the researcher wants to explore this question, how he or she will do it, and what it means to the researcher and the intended audience.

3. *Background/statement of the problem/significance of the project*—Be succinct. Clearly support the statement with documentation and references and include a review of the literature. This section presents and summarizes the problem intended to be solved and the proposed solution to that problem. What is the question the researcher wants to explore in the research and why is this an interesting and important question? In thinking about the significance, the researcher takes the position of an educated newspaper reader. If she or he were to see an article about the research in the paper, how would s/he explain the importance of the project?
4. *Experimental/Project Design*—Design and describe a work plan for this project. This section of the proposal should explain the details of the proposed plan. How will the researcher go about exploring the

research question? What will be the methods? What does the researcher see as the major issue to explore? (example: What constitutes a credible curriculum for middle and high-school students to resist vaping? What information will parents/guardians, teachers, and students need to develop a strong campaign against vaping at the middle and high-school levels?)

Be specific about what will be done in the plan. The reasoning behind the research opportunity is to be sure that the researcher has a meaningful experience. If the reviewer cannot tell what part of a project the researcher will be doing, he/she cannot evaluate the experience.

5. *Project timeline*—Give an overview of when the researcher is going to act on specific steps of the project. This does not need to be a day-to-day list but, depending on the length of the project, it may give a weekly or monthly overview. Be sure to include time to review/synthesize data or to reflect on the experience and time to make the final report or write a final paper.
6. *Anticipated results/final products and dissemination*—Describe the final product. A final product will include the publishable manuscript of the action research and an indication of how the project will be presented to an intended audience. This section may also include an interpretation and explanation of results as related to the question; a discussion on or suggestions for further work that may help address the problem trying to be solved; an analysis of the expected impact of the scholarly or creative work on the audience; or a discussion on any problems that could hinder a creative endeavor.

These directives not only help the researcher write a submitted proposal for the study, but will also plan how the study will be undertaken and what results are anticipated. All researchers can have useful experiences planning and carrying out their action research by following these steps to develop their proposals.

A SAMPLE PROPOSAL

Maureen and Tony took more deliberate steps to design the proposal they would present to the principals of the middle and high schools. They recognized that expanding this initiative to the high-school level could expand the workload in their plan, but they felt the extra work would have a greater impact on students, families, and the community at large.

Maureen and Tony's Proposal—a Sample to Follow

Maureen and Tony created the following proposal that was shared with the principals of both the elementary and high schools. This sample proposal followed the six steps suggested for the design of an effective proposal.

The Proposal

Curtailing the use of tobacco in public schools has been in the forefront of legislation since the 1990s. Tobacco use was moved to outside the building—so many feet away from students as an initial step to prevent young people from forming a nicotine addiction. With vaping as an alternative to smoking tobacco, schools are once again facing health and safety issues of its students.

According to an article in *Newsweek*,[2] The New Nicotine Addiction: U.S. Teen Vaping Stats Spike in 2018, the FDA reported findings that more than 1.3 million high-school students use e-cigarettes in 2018 compared to 2017. In December of 2020, the National Institute on Drug Abuse[3] reported the following statistics (see table 10.1).

Informal surveys of parents, guardians, and teachers revealed that awareness of the nationwide epidemic in vaping was minimal. Teachers in the schools admitted suspecting that middle and high-school students were vaping in the bathrooms both during and after school hours. Parents and guardians were not aware of the situation in the schools. Students at the middle and high-school levels reported vaping as a daily occurrence in their schools.

The goal of this research was to promote programs that prevent the use of vaping among middle and high-school students. To reach this goal, an awareness program on vaping will be developed and implemented to provide information to middle and high-school students, parents/guardians, and teachers about the dangers of vaping that affects teens nationwide. The goal is to curtail incidences of teen vaping to defeat the vaping epidemic. The research question of focus is: What elements of a Vape Awareness Program that focuses on student, parent, and teacher awareness are essential in local elementary and high schools?

Table 10.1 Trends in Prevalence of Various Drugs for 8th, 10th, and 12th Graders, 2020 (in percent)*

	Time Period	8th Grade	10th Grade	12th Grade
Any Vaping	Lifetime	24.1	41	47.2
	Past Year	19.2	34.6	39
	Past Month	12.5	23.5	28.2

Since vaping among teens has increased in the past few years and since it is relatively a new topic, more learning for more learners is essential. Teaching students and parents about the dangers of vaping is vital to combat the teen vaping epidemic across our nation and prevalent in our local schools. Extensive research on the topic of teen vaping, the lack of an effective anti-vaping curriculum for our students, first-hand knowledge that teens were vaping in elementary and secondary schools supported the identification of these benefits of an anti-vaping awareness initiative.

We are proposing programs that comprise three key elements: (1) student awareness through a wellness curriculum; (2) parent/guardian awareness through workshops that feature medical, law enforcement, and community resources; and (3) teacher awareness through workshops on an anti-vaping curriculum.

Timeline: Eighteen Months Development and Implementation of Awareness Program (January 2020–June 2021)

January 2020: Town Hall Meeting including parents/guardians, faculty, local community members—conduct survey on current awareness of the dangers of vaping and soliciting volunteers for working on awareness program

February 2020: Middle and High-School Assemblies on vaping awareness; student survey on exposure and use of tobacco and vaping

March 2020: Organization of working committees including school personnel (teachers, administrators, staff), parents/guardians, middle and high-school students, local community resource personnel (medical, law enforcement, businesses)

April 2020: Review of survey data and analyzing data results; initial sub-committee ideas for formulating awareness programs and seeking needed funding

May–September 2020—Development of awareness programs: for students, parent/guardians (community), and teachers; researching current curriculum plans, faculty and staff professional development opportunities, and possible grants from the National Institutes of Health for developing and implementing the programs

October 2020—Full committee presentations on the awareness programs

November–December 2020—Review, edits, and updates to awareness programs with calendar dates for implementation

January 2021—Town Hall presentation of awareness programs with confirmed dates for presentations

February–April 2021—Implementation of three awareness programs

May 2021—Survey on program effectiveness to the three targeted groups; review of data from surveys and planning for next steps

June 2021—Sharing data and next steps to students, faculty, local community; planning for sharing programs beyond the local community

Because of the nature of this epidemic, we feel the community needs to be engaged with each part of this program. While school personnel will ultimately be responsible for teacher training and development of the anti-vaping curriculum for students, members of the community will make a valuable contribution to ideas for the implementation of these programs. We are working from the premise that it takes a village to raise a child—especially a healthy one.

As parents and teachers, and active members in the community, we will be looking for programs to promote a healthy mindset in students, their families, and the members of the community. While we are addressing the current issue of vaping, we hope to use the experience to unite a community for a common cause of health and safety and thus serve as a model for other communities who face similar challenges.

USING THE PROPOSAL

Maureen and Tony's proposal was the detailed plan for their action research. They clearly identified the problem facing the larger community regarding the vaping epidemic. They identified the goal of making students, parents/guardians, and the community aware of the dangers of vaping. They gave some background of the problem and expressed the importance of community-wide awareness of the vaping problem. They made a timeline that was realistic and outlined the steps they hoped to take to research an awareness program.

The proposal laid the groundwork for their action research plan. This action research plan was initially shared with the principals of the elementary and high schools within their town. Recognizing the importance of this initiative and receiving the endorsement of both principals, they presented the proposal to the parent advisory coordinator of both schools who in turn shared it with local council members who gave recommendations for engaging the community beyond the schools. Eventually this initiative by a parent who was a teacher became a statewide endeavor that currently has reached more than fifty schools. Action research is leadership. Leading up is focusing on possibilities beyond the problems.

NOTES

1. Crace, D. (2020, February 25). 7 steps for effective planning. *TakingPoint Leadership.* https://takingpointleadership.com/7-steps-for-effective-planning/

2. Birkenbuel, R. (2018, December 18). The New Nicotine Addiction: U.S. Teen Vaping Stats Spike in 2018. *Newsweek.* Retrieved June 6, 2021 from https://www.newsweek.com/new-nicotine-addiction-us-teen-vaping-stats-spike-2018-1262414

3. National Institute on Drug Abuse. (2020, Dec.). Tobacco/nicotine and vaping trends and statistics. *National Institutes of Health.* https://www.drugabuse.gov/drug-topics/tobacconicotine-vaping/tobacconicotine-vaping-trends-statistics

Chapter 11

EXECUTING-EVALUATING the Plan

How to Start Smart and End Smart

Know what you want to do, hold the thought firmly, and do every day what should be done, and every sunset will see you that much nearer to your goal.

—Elbert Hubbard

This chapter examines methods to implement the plan and determines its potential for success. Doing so helps leaders know and understand the potential effectiveness of the plan and how to improve the organization consciously and continuously. In this chapter, the reader will consider how SMART goals can lead to SMART plans and how gathered data is used to evaluate the plan. In this chapter, a pastor details how he executed his SMART action plan to determine the ways to meet the needs of an aging congregation.

PLANS, PLANNERS, AND PLANNING

A sense of urgency can be one of the greatest drivers toward success. But like many acts of consistency, acting on your goals every single day takes massive motivation and a strong sense of mission-driven commitment. Having a plan is the first step; executing the plan is the first goal.

Some folks are great planners. They thrive on the adrenalin surge they experience in the process of planning. They come to the planning meetings psyched and ready to get started. Their enthusiasm is contagious. But, when it comes to the implementation of the plan, they are nowhere to be found (except at another planning meeting.) What happened?

Dr. Melaine Wilson,[1] a psychologist and a homeschool mother of six, posted a similar question on her website PSYCHOWITH6: Why don't we follow through with our plans and goals? Wilson discloses that after five years of research she found three common reasons why people do not follow through with their plans: (1) planning reduces anxiety; (2) our subconscious knows the real reason we made plans; and (3) we do not know how we work best.

Wilson explains that when we set goals or make plans, the anxiety that moved us in that direction is decreased just by the very act of making the plan. Research shows that the act of planning tricks our brain into believing we have achieved the plan, so further action is not needed. We can relax until the anxiety peaks again.

She further explains that the real reason for our planning is not usually good enough. This is similar to the New Year resolutions we made to join the fitness club in an earlier chapter. Year after year, we plan to lose the same weight we lost last year right before the family wedding when we had to look good. The *why* for the plan is weak and therefore not motivating enough to make it happen.

Of all the reasons for not following through with the plan, Wilson says the one that has the greatest impact not knowing how we work best. We have mirror images of the way things work for someone else—getting up at 4:00 a.m. to write a chapter of the book because isn't that how Mary Higgins Clarke did it; adding so many additional steps each day to an exercise routine because that is how Cousin Bruce became a champion runner. Until we determine what works best for us, our own productivity formula, plans will remain as plans.

SMART GOALS, SMART PLANS

Everybody wants to be smart—smart people make things look easy. Looking smart is not enough; you need the motivation to take action with the smarts you have.

The history of SMART goals can be traced as far back as the end of the nineteenth century when American philosopher and writer Elbert Hubbard said, "Many people fail in life, not for lack of ability or brains or even courage, but simply because they have never organized their energies around a goal."[2] People needed a way to organize their efforts in a way that led to success.

This format became a reality when George T. Doran,[3] a consultant and former director of Corporate Planning for Washington Water Power Company, published his paper on the SMART way to write goals and objectives. In his 1981 paper he provided some directives:

How do you write meaningful objectives?—that is, how do you frame a statement of results to be achieved? Managers are confused by all the verbiage from seminars, books, magazines, consultants, and so on. Therefore, when it comes to writing effective objectives, corporate officers, managers, and supervisors just have to think of the acronym SMART. Ideally speaking, each corporate, department and section objective should be SMART.[4]

Doran's original SMART definition included five criteria:

- Specific: target a specific area for improvement.
- Measurable: quantify, or at least suggest, an indicator of progress.
- Assignable: specify who will do it.
- Realistic: state what results can realistically be achieved given available resources.
- Time-related: specify when the result can be achieved.

Doran saw that by helping people focus on these five areas, their chances of success increased. Over the years, words have been substituted in the acronym, and even added to SMARTER[5]—with two additional criteria that support the L.E.A.D.E.R. model:

- Evaluated: appraisal of a goal to assess the extent to which it has been achieved.
- Reviewed: reflection and adjustment of your approach or behavior to reach a goal.

We will briefly look at each of the criteria of the SMART goal using a pastor's study of his aging congregation by considering a virtual church as a viable alternative to a brick-and-mortar church.

SMART GOALS FOR A SMART CHURCH

When starting with a goal, the first criterion is to be specific about what is wanted. If the goal is ambiguous, one never will ever know if the goal was attained. If the goal is stated as *I want to start a virtual church*, that may be a lofty goal. However, if the goal is stated as *I want in the next five months to determine the spiritual experiences preferred by elderly congregants when they are unable to attend the actual church building for services and plan those experiences before the winter season*, that goal has much more specificity.

Once the goal is specific, determine a way to measure the goal. Because this goal has two objectives: (1) determine the spiritual experiences preferred by elderly congregants and (2) plan for those preferred experiences, two measures will be necessary. To determine the preferences of the elderly, a survey completed by at least 50 percent of the elderly congregants would be a viable measure of the preferences of this group. The second measure would be a planned implementation of those preferences prior to the start of the winter season.

Both the goal and the measure must be attainable. Lofty goals and good measures are only as effective as they are attainable. In executive leadership, this most often reflects the effectiveness of the whole enterprise. As in all aspects of leadership, the lone ranger approach will not work. In this scenario, it is not just the pastor who impacts the congregation. It is not just the pastor who will carry out this plan. The plan will only be attainable if the congregation has a way to survey the elderly, to review the survey results, to involve the service ministers in planning alternative experiences, and to provide the experiences to the satisfaction of the elderly. A team of committed individuals will make this possible.

The goal must be relevant or realistic for the organization. Setting a goal of meeting the needs of 100 percent of the elders in the congregation is unrealistic and will lead to failure. Survey results of 50 percent are considered excellent, while survey results of 5–30 percent are more typical. The goal needs to be reasonably controlled. Be sure the goal is relevant to the organization. Providing for an aging congregation is relevant if the church will continue to exist into the future.

The goal must be timebound. Without a set time limit, the goal may never be achieved because there is no endpoint in mind. Establishing a time frame sets restrictions and adds pressure to accomplish the goal by an established endpoint. Having a beginning and endpoint allows for continuous review of accomplishments and determining interim goals to make the end goal possible. Figure 11.1 provides an overview of this SMART plan.

EXECUTING THE PLAN

As stated previously, creating the plan is the first step. Implementing the plan is the first accomplishment. Using the SMART format addresses Wilson's[6] three points for why individuals often do not accomplish plans and goals. Getting the plan down on paper addresses the adrenalin rush. Enthusiasm often accompanies this aspect of planning, enthusiasm makes the plan possible.

In the case of this pastor and congregation, the why of the plan is clear: the majority of the congregation is elderly and if the congregation wants to continue to be viable, that majority will be important to the survival and

SPECIFIC target a specific area for improvement	In the next five months determine the spiritual experiences preferred by elderly congregants when they are unable to attend the actual church building for services and plan for those experiences before the winter season begins.
MEASURABLE quantify, or at least suggest, an indicator of progress	A 50% survey response from the elders will provide an overview of needs. Implement preferred experiences at least three times before winter begins.
ATTAINABLE specify who will do it	A congregational team will create and conduct surveys, review survey results, and share results with congregation's services team. The congregation's services team will plan and deliver preferred experiences prior to Advent.
REALISTIC/RELEVANT state what results can realistically be achieved given available resources.	Because the congregation continues to serve an ever-increasing elderly population, consideration must be made for how to provide for their spiritual needs when they are unable to attend the church building for services. With the majority of the congregation moving toward 65+, the other members of the congregation must make plans to continue the elderly's involvement in the church community by providing for their spiritual needs.
TIME-BOUND specify when the result can be achieved	Mid-January – planning meeting with congregational team February (March) – conduct surveys April-May – review survey results June – share survey results with Services Team July-September – plan experiences for elderly October-November – hold at least 3 experiences

Figure 11.1   SMART Plan for Alternative Church Experiences.

continuance of the congregation. Wilson's second reason for plans not working (the why of the plan is weak and therefore not a good enough reason for it to happen) has already been addressed by the pastor and at least some members of the congregation. The why—providing for the spiritual needs of the elderly in the congregation who may be prevented from coming to the church building—relates to the mission and vision of the church. This church's mission statement—helping all find their way to God and others—is the why for keeping the elders connected.

Wilson's third point—not knowing how we work best—is the area of challenge for any organization. A fundamental disposition for transforming was presented in the chapter on continuous improvement: "transforming an organization requires the disposition and desire to make the organization become more of what it intends to be. The mission, the vision, and the hopes for the organization form the road map to 'arrive where we started.'"[7]

While an organization is made up of many and diverse individuals, the reason for coming together determines more about how the group works best.

In the case of this congregation, helping all find their way to God and others was more than just the mission statement framed in the vestibule of the church. This organization had mirror images of what could work, but they recognized that the congregation was an organization of individuals who may have different ways to get to an end goal, but what they had in common was the vision of the goal.

In the case of a congregation, these are people who are neither bound by a forty-hour workweek for the church, nor by the constraints of losing a job, nor of going this alone. One common element in congregations is the choice of belonging. As this congregation established their SMART plan, their common goal was front and center and using the SMART planning format, they discovered how they could work best together.

Together they believed—collective efficacy—that they could determine how to measure progress toward the goal, who would be responsible for moving toward that goal, what they planned to accomplish, and when they would see the goal become a reality. The SMART plan led to an even smarter church.

EVALUATING THE PLAN WITH DATA

One of the scariest parts of research in general, and action research in particular, is data. What is it? How do I find it? What do I do with it once I find it? How does data make a difference in the research?

Dave Turek,[8] the guy who developed the supercomputer at IBM, calculated that from the year 2003 and going back to the beginning of time, humanity generated five exabytes—that's five billion gigabytes—of information. He noted that the previous year they were cranking out that much data every two days, and by the following year they would be doing that every ten minutes. Keep in mind, that was a decade ago. Imagine how much data is generated today.

Data can be overwhelming. The SMART plan that identifies the needed data upfront takes a giant step forward in executing a viable plan. Review once again what this congregation determined would be the measurable part of this plan as noted in figure 11.2.

MEASURABLE quantify, or at least suggest, an indicator of progress	1. A 50% survey response from the elders will provide an overview of needs. 2. Implement preferred experiences at least three times before winter begins

Figure 11.2   Measurable Data.

In this case, some data was already established from previous church records. The records held names, addresses, dates of birth, membership in the congregation, significant dates affiliated with life events within the church—baptisms, marriages, funerals, burials. This was how the pastor knew that more than 50 percent of the congregants were sixty-five years of age or older. Weekly church attendance records revealed who was present in the pews and provided insight into the number of elderly congregants who were not in attendance on a regular basis.

This data—the baseline data—provided the setting for this situation. This data provided an overview of the current situation that indicated the congregation was moving in an unexpected direction. This data most likely unfolded the question—what are we going to do about this?

In developing the SMART plan, the planners could not turn back time but wanted this problem to be a gateway to the desired future—they were leading up! They glimpsed a future possibility to permit all members of the congregation—even those who were unable to physically attend in the church building—to attend. With the baseline data in place, the planners determined two essential forms of data: what the elders needed to continue their spiritual development and what the service team could provide to spiritual development.

While other data such as reasons the elders were not in physical attendance may have been of interest, collecting the data to move toward the goal was more essential. To decide which data are necessary, keep in mind that for all data collected, the data needs to be analyzed and interpreted to be of use. Does the organization have the personnel to handle all the data?

When considering the data for any case, stay focused on what the data collected will contribute to answering the research question. The question for this congregation was: *What are the spiritual experiences preferred by our elderly congregants when they are unable to attend the actual church building for services and how can we provide for those preferred experiences before the next winter season?* The data collection would be in the form of a survey for all the elders. That data would generate the possible action steps for providing spiritual experiences before the start of another winter season where church attendance by the elderly was at its lowest.

THE PLAN UNFOLDS

One aspect of the SMART plan is the built-in timetable that focuses on the plan. For the congregation seeking insights on how to meet the spiritual needs of its elders, the timebound activities kept the organization on track to accomplish its goal (see figure 11.3).

TIME-BOUND specify when the result can be achieved	Mid-January – planning meeting with congregational team
	February (March) – conduct surveys
	April-May – review survey results
	June – share survey results with Services Team
	July-September – plan experiences for elderly
	October-November – hold at least 3 experiences

Figure 11.3   Timebound Plan.

Having an overview of the intended plan gave participants deadlines to meet. At the initial meeting in January, the congregational team recognized the need to conduct surveys in February and possibly into March to reach the first goal of a 50 percent return rate of the surveys. But prior to conducting surveys, the team needed to determine the data they wanted from the survey. The intended data would guide them to find a survey that would adequately collect the information they wanted or help them realize that adapting a survey to include their own questions would be more beneficial.

Another challenge in planning for the survey included how they would reach the elderly with the survey. The first means of reaching the elderly was through a survey sent by mail to each of the elderly in the parish. That required verifying mailing addresses and the number of elderly at each household so that each person received a survey. To prepare the elderly with an awareness of the upcoming survey, the team created a telephone relay announcing the arrival of the survey within the next two weeks.

Additionally, the team shared that members of the congregation would be available to help elderly members complete the survey with telephone or electronic support, an in-person visit, or by reading the survey to the individual and completing the survey for the elder with the answer the elder provided. All mailed surveys contained a self-addressed stamped envelope for returning the completed survey.

February and March were designated as the months for completing the surveys. Members of the congregation volunteered to help the team collect the surveys in-person as visitors or with online support for those who needed it.

One other level of planning took place with the creation of the survey. The team was unable to find a survey that met the data needs they initially identified. While they found some survey questions that targeted the intended data, additional questions were added to the survey. To keep the survey basic, the team created a survey with ten questions using Likert-scale responses for the closed-ended questions and five open-ended questions that targeted the preferences of the elderly in meeting their spiritual needs. They piloted the survey with congregants between the ages of sixty and sixty-four to find out if the survey was readable, understandable, and easy to complete.

The timeline for the first months of this case required specific actions to create a survey, send the survey, and collect the survey results. The team in the congregation accepted responsibility for the survey. The pastor, the choir, the music ministers, the servers, the fellowship team were deliberate in their actions to move forward. Recognizing that they would be responsible for planning for the needs of the elderly and creating services to respond to those needs, they began by anticipating what the needs might be and how they could respond to those needs within the time frame.

This anticipated planning included ways they could bring Bible studies, communion, and prayer experiences to those unable or uncomfortable in attending their brick-and-mortar church. They did not want to just wait to see what the surveys would reveal, but rather, wanted to jump-start planning these services.

WHAT THE DATA REVEALED

While the team had a 43 percent return rate on the surveys by the end of March, a part of the team began to review the data they received while another group continued contacting elders who had not responded. They wanted to reach the targeted 50 percent of the elders. Reviewing the Likert-type responses was easier as the quantitative information provided specific responses to questions about types of services meaningful to the elders. Among those that had a highly important rating were: scripture sharing, fellowship, intercessory prayer, communion, the weekly homily, and the music.

It was more challenging to examine open-ended responses to questions such as (1) What do you miss most when you are not able to come to church? and (2) What would you want to receive from the church at times when you cannot be present? These qualitative responses required additional teasing of the responses to look for common themes.

> I can pray at home, and I do. But it is just not the same as when I am with my friends and we are all together praying at the same time.
>
> I miss who counts on my prayers. In our general intercessions we pray for those who are sick, or for those who lost loved ones, and we pray for those in the church who have died. When I'm not there, I don't know any of this and I feel badly that I can't be praying for others who need me.
>
> Our weekly services are a highlight of the week for me. I look forward to being with other people and visiting with them and sharing fellowship even after the service.

I am so lonely when I do not get to go to church. During the winter months I
   hardly go anywhere so I am alone most of the time.
One thing (please don't laugh) that I really miss when I can't go to church is
   the physical movement. You know we stand up, then sit down, we join in
   rhythm with the choir. I never really thought about church as a workout—but
   that is part of it too.
The church has an environment that gives me peace of mind. The lights, the
   candles, the music—all of that feeds my soul. I don't have that at home as I
   live with my daughter and her five kids. It is always noisy—even at night. I
   miss that peace of mind.

As the team reviewed the data from the survey, they noticed that the
quantitative data gave them the information they expected to hear from the
elders—the types of services that would feed them spiritually. The services
team anticipated some of the responses to the open-ended questions. The
open-ended questions contributed description information to the closed-
ended survey questions.

The data from the open-ended questions surprised the team. The responses
in those questions gave greater insight into the spirit of the elders—what
made them a part of the community and how physical presence contributed
to that spirit and how non-presence left them without that spirit. That data
provided a more focused response to the question: *What are the spiritual
experiences preferred by our elderly congregants when they are unable to
attend the actual church building for services and how can we provide for
those experiences before the next winter season?*

The qualitative data from the open-ended questions allowed elderly members of the congregation to express the value of the services to them—scripture sharing, communion, intercessory prayer, the homily. But these rituals
were only a part of what the elders missed. In planning experiences for the
elders who were unable to attend church physically, the ambiance had to be
captured, the fellowship had to have a place, and the elders had to have a
presence among the congregation. Planning for that full spiritual experience
would take much more than planning services. The data spoke volumes.

OTHER ISSUES TO CONSIDER IN EXECUTING
AND EVALUATING THE PLAN

Action research can effectively be used by most organizations. Keep in mind
that the research needs to be a tightly focused study (this is not meant to be
a scientific experiment that will alter life forms!), with the main intent of the

continuous improvement of the organization and its transformation into more of what it intends to be.

With that being said, action research comes under the same legal and ethical requirements as any scientific research that involves human subjects. While the debate continues regarding the extent that action researchers are subject to the Code of Federal Regulations for the Protection of Human Subjects—also known as 45 CFR 46—all organizations are subject to the code of protecting the rights and well-being of human subjects.

When conducting action research, while a formal Internal Review Board decision may not be required in some settings, all organizations are required to abide by the legal and ethical codes of conduct in their contract. Whenever possible, it is appropriate to seek permission from the administration for conducting any type of research.

A full disclosure of the research process, the reason for conducting the research, and how the research findings will be shared are advisable. Guaranteeing the anonymity of participants and information that can lead to identifying the participants should be established before the research begins. The requirements of the organization must be followed in all circumstances—especially in using data from a study.

These precautions should not impede researchers from practicing self-reflection, a major reason for doing action research. Action research requires a series of commitments. It is a journey of the self through reflective inquiry that is social to improve an organization and self. Circumstances and understandings of personal, professional, and political dimensions are aspects of action research.[9,10] This reflection has the potential to lead to significant growth for the researcher and the organization.

NOTES

1. Wilson, M. (2018, Dec. 4). *Why you aren't following through on your plans and goals*. PSYCHOWITH6. https://psychowith6.com/why-you-arent-following-through-plans-goals/

2. Elbert Hubbard Quotes. (n.d.). BrainyQuote.com. Retrieved May 3, 2021, from BrainyQuote.com Web site: https://www.brainyquote.com/quotes/elbert_hubbard_121477

3. Doran, G. T. (1981). There's a S.M.A.R.T. way to write management's goals and objectives. *Management Review*, *70*(11), 35–36.

4. Doran, There's a S.M.A.R.T. way, 35.

5. Haughey, D. (2014, Dec. 13). *A brief history of SMART goals*. ProjectSmart. https://www.projectsmart.co.uk/brief-history-of-smart-goals.php

6. Wilson, *Following through on your plans*.

7. Jacobs, S. M. A., and Kushner, S. R. (2017). *How can you become the boss?: From personal mastery to organizational transformation.* Rowman & Littlefield, 133.

8. Turek, D. (2012). The case against digital sprawl. *Business Week*, 2. Retrieved May 10, 2021 from Bloomberg: https://www.bloomberg.com/news/articles/2012-05 -02/the-case-against-digital-sprawl

9. Kemmis, S. (2010). Research for praxis: Knowing doing. *Pedagogy, Culture & Society, 18*(1), 9–27.

10. Kemmis, S. (2011). Researching educational praxis: Spectator and participant perspectives. *British Educational Research Journal, 38*(6), 885–905.

Chapter 12

REPEATING the Steps as Needed

Though nobody can go back and make a new beginning,
anyone can start over and make a new ending.

—Chico Xavier

Mertler viewed action research as a cyclical process in *Action Research: Teachers as Researchers in the Classroom*:

> That is to say, whereas action research has a clear beginning, it does not have a clearly defined endpoint. Ordinarily, teacher-researchers design and implement a project, collect and analyze data in order to monitor and evaluate the project's effectiveness, and then make revisions and improvements to the project for future implementation.[1]

This chapter directs the reader to review what has been learned in the action research process and to take the next steps toward continuous improvement. The leader uses what has been learned to plan the next steps for the transformation of the organization and to share the learning with other colleagues.

TWO LEVELS OF LEARNING

The action researcher and those who read the research learn two lessons: (1) lessons related to the problem addressed in the research and (2) lessons about the research process. In action research, a member of the organization is the researcher, unlike most scientific research where the subject is often studied by outsiders.

While scientific research is profitable and objective, the insights of the participants in the research are often disregarded and not included in the study.

With the organization as the researcher, insights into the problem of the study are more fully developed and contribute to the findings and applications for the next steps in the learning and the reflective process.

LEARNING FROM THE RESEARCH PROBLEM

The *L.E.A.D.E.R.* steps in the action research process lead the researcher in a clearly prescribed format with an equally clear identification of the problem under study. The problem identifies a disconnect in the alignment chain (figure 12.1) in the organization. As Trevor and Varcoe[2] explained, the chain connects the organization's purpose—the what and why of what it does to the organization's business strategy—what the organization is trying to win at to fulfill its purpose, its organizational capability—what it is good at to win, its resource architecture—what makes the organization good, and the management system—what delivers the winning performance.

Once the disconnect is identified with any link in the chain, the researcher examines what s/he knows about that link in the chain.

The next step in the process involves the researcher in finding what other researchers learned through their studies of similar problems. Based on knowledge about the organization and the research from other studies, the researcher devises a plan of action to address the problem, and then puts the plan in action to address the problem.

Once the plan has been implemented, the researcher now faces the challenge of determining whether the problem has been solved. In addition to finding out if the problem has been solved, the action researcher decides the next steps to take with the problem and communicates the findings of the study to the organizational community.

HAS THE PROBLEM BEEN SOLVED?

Individuals in an organization who undertake the challenge to solve a problem are actively seeking a solution, they are looking beyond the problem to

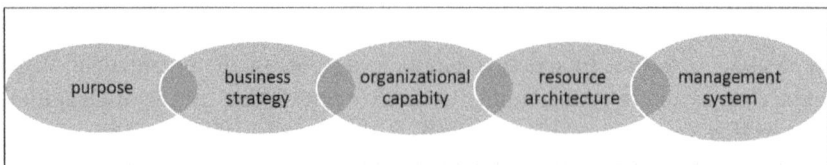

Figure 12.1   Alignment Chain.

the possibilities the solution may present. The researcher recognizes that the disconnects among the organization's purpose, strategy, capability, architecture, or management system must be resolved. No one is out to fail, and when a problem persists, failures on the part of anyone or anything in the organization are an uncomfortable reality.

But the counter reality is welcoming. No one will work harder at resolving an organizational problem than the members of the team who recognize the problem. The team will also be the first to recognize if the problem has been solved or if alternative solutions must be considered. They see the problem as a gateway to something better, not a desire to return to what was.

QUESTIONS TO CONSIDER

When the plan for resolving the problem in the action research has been implemented, the researcher needs to consider the possible next steps. Two questions guide this process: (1) Should the research be continued? or (2) If the research was conducted again, what would the researcher do differently?

Should the Research Be Continued?

In returning to the original question for this part of the research—was the problem solved?—the answer in the negative would generate a positive answer to the question—should the research be continued? The researcher determines whether the problem has been solved and must consider viable next steps.

This was the case for a non-profit food pantry and thrift store that served the needs of a local community since 1972. As with most non-profit organizations, this organization faced the challenge of balancing business with benevolence to fulfill its mission. The thrift store was the primary economic engine, relying on donations and volunteers from the community.

Additionally, the organization conducted four primary fundraisers throughout the year. The food pantry was stocked with items that individuals and families could have on an as-needed basis and the community café served a continental breakfast and lunch Mondays through Fridays. There was always a place at the table because there was no charge to those who were fed, although donations were always welcomed.

The impact on the community increased every year—the kitchen served 700,000 meals served 2019 and over one million meals in 2020! The extensive increase in the number of meals served in 2020, while greatly beneficial, hit the business aspect of the organization with financial challenges.

In the midst of a pandemic, the fiscal and effectiveness challenges needed immediate attention. The hungry cannot wait for board meetings or for additional fundraisers to occur, or for a donation from an unexpected donor. The organization's leaders and stakeholders recognized a need to set an organizational map for the future. It was up to the leadership to spearhead initiatives to keep the doors open, the consumers happy, and the volunteers returning to work on a daily basis.

It took a pandemic for the organization to start mapping for the future. For nearly fifty years, this organization was able to *feed the hungry and clothe the naked.* Most of this endeavor was accomplished through the community pool of volunteers.

The thrift store was the money maker that supported the purchase of food for the pantry and the café. With the onset of the pandemic, income from the thrift store declined while the need for meals increased. Marion Mills, the volunteer executive director, knew the current business model of buying food to give it away was not viable.

After three months into the pandemic, the number of those needing breakfast and/or lunch doubled. The revenue from the thrift store was cut by 45 percent. With more mouths to feed and with fewer resources for buying food—short of the multiplication of the loaves and fishes—this valuable and needed community resource was facing extinction.

The staff of the executive director and the two part-time employees began working on the plan to do more with less. After using the band-aid approach, the first months of the pandemic—wait and hope for needed resources—the staff began plans to develop the organization's capacity building for productivity and effectiveness. Working with its nearly eighty volunteers, they began to examine their human and organizational assets to implement effective policies, programs, and practices. These assets included fiscal resources, processes, institutional knowledge, leadership, and relationships.

The executive team saw "capacity building" as an ongoing, evidence-informed process used to develop an organization's potential to be productive and effective. From its inception, this organization was crafted with and supported by the richness of its volunteers. If the organization was going to create lasting organizational change, a series of action steps and complementary strategies—assessment, strategic planning, and information sharing—had to incorporate the talents of its volunteer pool.

Because of restrictions on public gatherings and the inability to serve meals in confined spaces, the first change had to be replacing sit-down meals with grab-and-go. Serving breakfast and lunch from 8:30 a.m. to 1:00 p.m. Monday to Friday meant serving approximately 2,700 meals a day prior to the pandemic. Volunteers were on hand to wash the tables, reset the serving places, and replenish condiments. Volunteers have often maintained a system of entrance and exit to the café to accommodate the number of people they fed. The switch to grab-and-go made marked changes.

The most obvious change was in the number of on-demand meals. With the onset of the pandemic, the daily distribution rose to 3,800 meals a day. The continental breakfast remained similar in offerings to the pre-pandemic breakfast, but the lunch menu changed substantially. Because of the grab-and-go nature, soup or salad and sandwich and fruit and a beverage became the norm. Former entrees included baked ziti, or stew, or chicken pot pie, but grab-and-go lunches necessitated packaged selections. Breakfast and lunch were brown bag pickups. The distribution of the meals was actually easier in this format, more people were fed, and the hours of operation could be reallocated for the volunteers.

One of the beneficial changes to this was the donation of food. Local vendors were more strategic with their donations (produce suppliers knew that fruit was in high demand for distribution, restaurants were able to donate surplus soup, and the local markets focused on products needed for sandwiches and for the packaging needed for this type of distribution).

The food donations increased substantially from the local community. Whereas previously the largest source of revenue came from the thrift store, now the donations focused on food supplies. The volunteers did not need to do the same amount of banking, shopping, and maintaining of the café. Their services could be used elsewhere. While the revenue amounts did not increase to meet the growing demand for meals, streamlined food donations eliminated other demands on time and the organization's assets.

At the other end of the spectrum, the organization had not solved the ongoing revenue challenge. When the pandemic slowly subsided, the return to what had been the norm was tempting. However, lessons were learned.

If the Research Was Conducted Again, What Would the Researcher Do Differently?

Starting over is not what any researcher wants to do. The hours, effort, and planning spent in the research process seemed a waste of time to the researcher. And yet what has been learned in that process is invaluable.

The executive team recognized aspects of this action research over which they had no control. The data included the number of meals distributed, the financial balance during the pandemic, and the number of volunteers who worked to ensure effective meal distribution.

While data had always been collected on meals served, the budget for income and expenses, and the number in the volunteer pool who donated hours, the urgency in this matter required the executive team to plan strategically with unknown demands. The data continued to be collected and what the data revealed gave insights into what this research showed.

During the first six months, while the meal numbers increased, changes began to happen in the total food cost. By the fourth month, the actual cost was slightly less than the estimated cost (see table 12.1).

This trend continued in the next three months. Another change was the number of volunteers needed to prepare and distribute meals. Prepandemic, the center required approximately fifteen volunteers daily to provide meals and run the thrift store. Because of the changes in the ways meals were provided, the number of volunteers almost doubled. With the exception of one or two volunteers who serviced the thrift store, all other volunteers were needed to prepare and distribute the meals to the ever-increasing numbers.

By the seventh month, positive changes were noted. While numbers of meals continued to increase, the difference between the estimate for what each meal should cost based on the cost of the previous year ($1.93 per plate for breakfast and $2.87 per plate for lunch) and the actual cost now was decreasing. So was the number of needed volunteers (see table 12.2).

Upon a quick review, the problem of sustaining the organization—even in a pandemic—seemed to be moving closer to closing the gap, reaching for possibilities of surviving and even thriving! If the research were done again, what would the executive team do differently? Several new questions arose. Is a pick-up-and-go meal a better option? Are fewer meal choices more effective? Can the organization provide more meals to more people with fewer options? How can the volunteers be utilized more effectively? This is the strategy behind big box stores like Costco. Giving customers fewer choices made their choices easier to make.[3]

RECOGNIZING VARIABLES OF THE STUDY

Before drawing any conclusions about the study, the executives realized that they had to consider the variables in the study and how the variables affected drawing conclusions that could be generalized for other populations. The team created a list of variables that were critical to this study.

The pandemic was a definite variable. Prior to the pandemic, the thrift store was the major financial supplier. Restrictions with the pandemic prohibited donations; thus, the supplies were limited. Meal planning and distribution totally changed. Eating within the center was prohibited, yet there were still people to feed.

Another variable was the types of meals. With the grab-and-go setup, the breakfast was continental—cereal, fruit, pastry, bagel, egg sandwiches, and milk or a hot beverage. Lunch included soup, sandwiches or salads, or a pasta

Table 12.1 Data during First Six Months of the Pandemic

	May	June	July	August	September	October
Breakfast	40,540	41,009	40,321	37,976	37,987	39,897
Est. cost	$78,242.20	$79,147.37	$77,819.53	$73,293.68	$73,314.91	$77,001.21
Lunch	45,213	46,187	48,143	44,879	48,005	51,994
Est. cost	$127,952.79	$130,709.21	$136,244.69	$127,007.57	$135,854.15	$147,143.02
Total Estimate Food Costs	$206,194.99	$209,856.58	$214,064.22	$200,301.25	$209,169.06	$224,144.23
Actual Food Costs	$209,345.56	$212,459.68	$214,287.63	$200,009.23	$208,442.90	$222,887.01
Diff	$3,150.57	$2,603.10	$223.41	$292.02	$726.16	$1,257.22
Volunteers per day	28	28	28	26	25	22

Table 12.2   The Second Six Months of the Pandemic

	November	December	January	February	March	April
Breakfast	42,783	43,776	43,005	41,983	38,897	38,929
Est. cost	*$82,571.19*	*$84,487.68*	*$82,999.65*	*$81,027.19*	*$75,071.21*	*$75,132.97*
Lunch	53,756	56,312	54,045	55,137	51,694	50,094
Est. cost	*$152,129.48*	*$159,362.96*	*$152,947.35*	*$156,037.71*	*$146,294.02*	*$141,766.02*
Total Estimate Food Costs	*$234,700.67*	*$243,850.64*	*$235,947.00*	*$237,064.90*	*$221,365.23*	*$216,898.99*
Actual Food Costs	*$228,084.76*	*$233,922.90*	*$226,455.89*	*$227,001.89*	*$210,708.34*	*$207,899.23*
Diff	*$6,615.91*	*$9,927.74*	*$9,491.11*	*$10,063.01*	*$10,656.89*	*$8,999.76*
Volunteers per day	20	16	15	13	13	13

dish, a sweet treat (cookies, Rice Krispy Treats, Granola bars) fruit, and a beverage. An assembly line format for packing meals was the norm.

One other variable in this study was the way the volunteers spent their time. Previous to the pandemic, fifteen volunteers committed to one day a week. The volunteers would work in the thrift store or would help with the meals—preparing the meals, serving the meals, cleaning up after the meals, shopping for food and supplies.

Because the meals were now streamlined, the many community merchants could be more deliberate with their donations. The increase in foods such as fruit made it possible to provide fruit daily, and sometimes for both meals. This made the daily cost of meals decline as the merchants focused their donations on foods that could be used immediately.

DETERMINING LIMITATIONS OF THE STUDY

Before presenting the findings of the study to other audiences, the researcher considers the limitations of the study. Creswell describes limitations as "potential weaknesses or problems with the study identified by the researcher. . . . they often relate to inadequate measures of variables, loss or lack of participants, small sample sizes, errors in measurement, and other factors typically related to data collection and analysis."[4]

Findings in action research are generally only relevant to the situation of the researcher. With that being said, this does not mean that findings from the study are so limited within the topic researched that no one else can benefit from the study. That is definitely not the case.

When considering the limitations of the study, the researcher acknowledges those areas in the study that may cause the study to lack generalizable results. In this study, the executive team recognized and acknowledged that the response of the community in their donations may not always be as generous outside of a pandemic. They also recognized that the donations became more specific—fruit, bread, beverages, paper products—in response to the center's deliberate donation list.

The executive team did not have ample time to create a strategic plan. The plan was for an immediate need with restrictions beyond their control. The volunteer pool was reorganized and had the training to fulfill an immediate need. Several volunteers increased their days and hours of service to meet the needs of the situation.

In reporting the findings of the study, the executive team moved from focusing on how to keep the program effective to reflecting on how the mission was alive in even these desperate times. A major focus of the findings was on the role of volunteers in making the center a place that responded not only during a pandemic, but at all times. *Always a place at the table* became a mantra for those served and those serving.

The executive team suggested that certain aspects of this action research plan needed to be repeated. They suggested further studies on the grab-and-go meal plan. If more people could be provided meals with this plan, should this be a viable option? If the cost of a meal could be reduced because community merchants knew which food and products to donate, should this format be considered? If volunteers could become specialists in one area of service, would this be a better use of personnel?

Beyond the focus on providing meals to many people, another area of consideration was how those who were served were impacted by the isolation of the pandemic. Pre-pandemic, people were seated at tables and had an opportunity for the community at least twice a day. Without this opportunity, what impact did this have on those served?

The financial data found that the center could actually do more with less. But the question remains: Is it worth it? Were recipients receiving nutritious and well-balanced meals? Was the center missing opportunities to receive other community donations because they were now restricting their types and varieties of meals? Were volunteers satisfied with how their time and talents were used? Would everything revert to the former ways of providing this service? The action research cycle continues.

DISSEMINATING THE FINDINGS

Disseminating findings from the study often occurs at the end of the study. Keen and Todres in their study on disseminating qualitative research findings noted:

> few authors of qualitative studies move beyond the dissemination of their work in the ubiquitous journal article. Though the number of qualitative projects increases year on year, the implications of this work appear to remain on shelves and have little impact on practice, research, policy, or citizens.[5]

If a problem was important enough to be studied, the findings are important enough to share with others who may have similar problems.

For researchers engaged in organizations such as non-profits, finding the time to write a scholarly article and then locate and submit the article for review by other researchers—who may not see the relevance of the problem or who are looking for the highly developed statistical-filled journal article—is not practical. The "ubiquitous journal article" is not the only way to share research findings. Keen and Tordes[6] identified three successful dissemination strategies:

(a) Tailor the approach to the audience in terms of content, message, and medium.
(b) Pay attention to the source of the message.
(c) Provide for active discussion of the findings.

AUDIENCE AWARENESS IN SHARING FINDINGS

The action researcher needs to consider the audiences that care about this problem and the findings from the study. Internal audiences would include those directly involved with the study and the participants in the study. This group would be within the organization.

Most likely the first audience will be the immediate supervisor or the executive team responsible for addressing the problem. This is generally the person(s) with whom the action researcher first discussed the problem and the proposed plan. If the problem is shared among several members of the organization, the community of researchers will be the first audience.

Beyond the first audience level, other audiences should be considered. The researcher considers all those within the organization immediately impacted by the problem. These could include department heads, secretarial staff, maintenance, and volunteers. The administration should receive regular updates on the study throughout the process. Updates can be in the form of emails, memos, and meetings, but should always be recorded in a written format for future reference.

Other personnel may be the next audience including community members beyond the organization. In this case that would include the recipients of the service, donors who support the service, other community members who are affiliated with the center. While this may not always be the case, many problems and findings do relate to settings beyond the walls of the organization, and the findings can be beneficial to the community at large.

The findings from action research should be made public and shared beyond the organization to contribute to the practice of the field. Groups beyond the immediate organization can include other non-profits with similar interests, local law enforcement that may need the information to continue their services, local businesses impacted by the organization. Any problem or solution that impacts others' needs to receive information about the research.

MEDIUM FOR SHARING FINDINGS

The medium the action researcher chooses to present findings will depend on the audience. When the findings of a study are shared within the organization where the study was conducted, all components of the study are contained and retained by the researcher. The elements that the researcher chooses to share with the selected audience will depend on how the findings will be used by the audience.

The findings from the study should be shared more extensively with those who are impacted the most. If the problem was an issue that affects changes in more than one department, the detailed sharing of methods and data collection and analysis will be more extensive.

For others within the organization who may want to use the methods in the study, the details of procedures and instruments may be very helpful. The data collected and analyzed may give insights for replicating the study, or for making adjustments to the organizational planning and processing.

While all the details of the study may be of great interest to other members of the organization, many of the findings will be of less interest to other staff members who may be more interested in the results and what actions will be taken to improve the current situation. An overview of results and next steps can be presented in a formal presentation during a department meeting or executive council.

In sharing the findings with other constituents—such as those served, board members, and benefactors—the confidentiality of data must be guarded. Presentations made to these groups may include a PowerPoint presentation, providing an overview of the study with general results from the study, and more clearly developed action steps that will be taken as a result of the findings from the study. Most of the times this audience level wants to know the answer to the question "So what? Now What?" Providing the "why and how" of what will happen as a result of the study is generally sufficient for this audience.

Sharing the results and findings of the study beyond the immediate organization generally requires different media. The action researcher decides what to share from the study based on the intended goals of the group. The sharing may take the form of an oral or visual presentation, a written report, and/or an electronic sharing through a blog, wiki, podcast, or newspaper or television broadcast.

Sharing results of the study at a district or state level is generally done through a more formal medium. A professional letter or report to board members or state representatives would most often be the medium, unless the research was part of a focused research initiated at these levels. While state officials may have some interest in research initiatives at the local level, the focus of action research undertaken by an organization generally does not require extensive sharing at that level.

Sharing results of action research with the larger community—beyond the organization and the local community most impacted by the research—may happen informally through popular social media such as Linkedin, Pinterest, or YouTube. More formalized sharing of action research is made through articles published in organizational literature and refereed journals. While not discounting the importance of this type of professional sharing, research conducted on a specific problem within an organization often does not have the personnel or time to engage in this type of publishing and would find the process challenging and time-consuming.

ACTIVE DISCUSSION OF THE FINDINGS

When using action research at the organizational level, an active discussion of the findings supersedes merely presenting the findings. Organizations consist of many constituents and these constituents have varying levels of interest in the problem addressed in the research. Actively discussing the findings of research invites constituents to consider the research, have a voice, and take a stand on the findings. For continuous improvement to happen, this kind of action in the research is critical.

Brookfield and Preskill relate their insights into the value of discussions:

> discussion is a valuable and inspiring means for revealing the diversity of opinion that lies just below the surface of almost any complex issue. Although there are many ways to learn, discussion is a particularly wonderful way to explore supposedly settled questions and to develop a fuller appreciation for the multiplicity of human experience and knowledge. To see a topic come alive as diverse and complex views multiply is one of the most powerful experiences we can have. . . . In a discussion where participants feel their views are valued and welcomed, it is impossible to predict how many contrasting perspectives will emerge or how many unexpected opinions will arise.[7]

To see action research in action, sharing findings by inviting insights into the research can shape the next steps in deciding which steps need to be repeated. When action research is viewed as a systematic way to move toward continuous improvement and bring about change, discussing the findings can only lead to multiple insights—which for those impacted by the change promotes self-reflective inquiry and collective efficacy leading to the transformation of the organization.

NOTES

1. Mertler, C. A. (2009). *Action research: Teachers as researchers in the classroom* (2nd ed.). Thousand Oaks, CA: Sage, 37.

2. Trevor, J. and Varcoe, B. (2017). How aligned is your organization? *Harvard Business Review*, *95*(1), 2–6.

3. Riangkrul, S. (2020, September 6). The winning Costco strategy. *Medium*. https://medium.com/the-innovation/the-winning-costco-strategy-19c2cb7c981

4. Creswell, J. W. (2008). *Educational research: Planning, conducting, and evaluating quantitative and qualitative research*. Upper Saddle River, NJ: Pearson Education, Inc., 207.

5. Keen, S. and Todres, L. (2007). Strategies for disseminating qualitative research findings: Three exemplars [36 paragraphs]. *Forum Qualitative Sozialforschung / Forum: Qualitative Social Research*, *8*(3), Art. 17, http://nbn-resolving.de/urn:nbn:de:0114-fqs0703174, Introduction

6. Keen and Todres, Strategies for disseminating qualitative research findings.

7. Brookfield, S. and Preskill, S. (1999). *Discussion as a way of teaching: Tools and techniques for university teachers*. McGraw-Hill Education (UK), 3.

Part III

PRACTICAL APPLICATION OF L.E.A.D.E.R. FOR LEADERS

Two questions remain with most forms of research: Where do you begin? and what do you do after the research is completed? In this part of the book, both questions will be addressed. The chapters in this part will include graphic organizers for developing the research and presenting the research to audiences.

These chapters will revisit the journey of action research and the expected commitments of the researcher. Action research as transformational leadership, collaborative efficacy, continuous improvement, and organizational transformation will be seen as the take-aways of action research. The next step is reflection for what will come next.

Chapter 13

Where to Start?

When you begin, you envision a better end but, when you get to the end, you see the beginning better!

—*Ernest Agyemang Yeboah*

Covey[1] proposed beginning with the end in mind, the logical path to begin action research. This chapter will revisit the initial consideration of the disconnect between expectation and reality and its frequent occurrence in any organization. The Town Council, the local hospital, the service organization, the family around the kitchen table can use the steps of the L.E.A.D.E.R. model to move from problems to possibilities, from complaining to collaborating to promote continuous improvement that leads to organizational transformation.

ACTION RESEARCH—AN EVERYDAY OCCURRENCE

Would it be right to say that every day is a day for action research? This may be true only on days when organizations face a problem—large or small—simple or wicked—which for most organizations is every day. If problems surface every day, where does the organization begin to deal with the problem?

Dissatisfaction with what-is, is the beginning of improvement. In action research, it is a step toward continuous improvement. It is a long and hard look at the discrepancy between expectation and reality. But it can also be moving us in the wrong direction.

Elizabeth Scott[2] invites readers to get out of the expectation versus reality trap. She notes that research studies reveal that the expectation of winning the lottery, finding the perfect spouse or job, or having that stellar bank account may only provide a temporary boost of happiness. She suggests that it is important to build an awareness of how your expectations stack up to reality.

When individuals go it alone in an organization, a blind spot is probably a reality. If the expectation is self-focused, the reality will most likely impact only the individual. This is Pip in Dicken's *Great Expectations*. When he conceives of something that is better than what he already has, he immediately desires the improvement. Much of what he desires is for himself and although these may be great expectations, the reality of what could be is more a dream.

Action research facilitates organizational change by collaborating with and involving the stakeholders in the entire process of diagnosis, problem identification, experiential learning, and the problem-solving process. Unlike Pip's, this focus is on the organization. The goal is moving from problem to possibility but moving collaboratively, efficaciously. The collaborative approach is followed when members of an organization consider a problem that impacts the organization, a problem that halts continuous improvement, that prevents seeing the possibility of transformation.

12 STEPS TO CHANGE

Why change? Change is hard. Our brains are wired for patterns—doing the same thing over and over. If you don't believe that humans are pattern seekers, consider the following: fold your hands with your fingers interlacing each other. Now move all those fingers so that what was on top is now on the bottom. How does that feel? Think about this—when you put on shoes or socks, you always start with the same foot. If you pick up the wrong shoe first, you instinctively put it down and reach for the "correct" shoe. Start noticing that. When you take your next shower, think about which hand holds the soap. Try changing it to the other hand. You may wonder if you actually got clean!

But change can be good. Change can make one more flexible. Change can help one see things in different ways. Change can get one out of a comfort zone and into new realities. And sometimes change is the only way out of a situation one does not want to be in.

Change can be intended or unintended. Intended change is what one hopes will happen, what one wants to have happened. Take for instance the idea behind email. Email was intended to be a simple way to communicate with people for purposes related to one's own goals, to stay connected, to be an alternative to making a phone call.

Then there is unintended change, the consequence, which is what actually happens. What happened with email was that spam, ads, and some nefarious activities took place to the extent that only about 10 percent of email actually accomplished its intended purpose. This was not the intended change email was supposed to make.

To produce the intended change, think of change as a process, not an event. Organizational change does not happen because one attended a training session, or because a new mandate came about, or because a new executive was hired. When experiencing change, one moves from what was known or done and transitions to a new way of knowing or doing.

In his blog *Change as a Process*, Tom Creasey[3] explains the change in three states: the current state, the transition state, and the future state. The current state is how things are at present: who constitutes the organization, how the processes work, and how the work is done. The current state is what works and what may not be working. But it is known by the group and thus is familiar and comfortable—this is how it's always been done. The transition state is that messy state that is often unorganized and in constant flux. It is the learning state as well as a challenging state. The future state is where the organization is going and because it is not established yet, it can be worrisome simply because it is unknown.

Creasey also notes that change should be considered from two levels: the individual and the organizational level. For each individual who goes through the change process, the individual also goes through a personal change process. And this change process is actualized in in all three states: current, transition, and future. Individuals need support in this change process to improve the organization. Individuals start the change process at different times and they take different amounts of time to move through the process. This reinforces that change is a process.

As for change at the organizational level, the challenge is meeting the needs of each individual while simultaneously letting the change process move forward. Knowing the right time to initiate a change—or a part of the change—can impact the whole process. For instance, in many change processes, employees need new skills and competencies to adapt to the day-to-day changes. However, initiating a training program when employees are still in the current state is not the optimal time to do this. Training would be better once employees have moved to the transition state. Knowing the process of change and how this process will unfold is necessary for making change happen.

In addition to the three states in the change process, consider who in the organization spends time in which state (see table 13.1). While all members of the organization spend time in each state, how they view change in each state dictates where they focus on the change process.[4]

Chapter 13

Table 13.1   Creasey's Organizational Employees and How They View the States of Change

	Current State	Transition State	Future State
Executives and senior leaders	What I need to change and why I am trying to implement change	A necessary evil to get me where I want to be	*The goal that I have decided to move my organization toward*
Project teams	What I'm starting with and must improve	*The focus of my daily work and what I'm charged with solving*	Where we ultimately want to end up
Front-line employees, managers, supervisors	*The day-to-day work that I do to deliver value to the organization*	A disorganized inconvenience to me doing my job	An unknown that may or may not be good for me

Senior leadership lives in the future state. They see where the organization should be six months to a year from now. The project teams live in the transition stage. They make the change happen by considering alternatives, proposing the plan, and taking needed steps. The front-line employees live in the present state. They do not stop what they are doing to implement change. They must keep going with the day-to-day happenings to sustain the organization while change happens.

The discrepancy among the three states can be catastrophic. Collaborative efficacy is what allows change to be a process rather than an event. The constant flow needed between leadership in action, collaborative efficacy, continuous improvement, and organizational transformation paints the picture for moving from problems to possibilities.

Figure 13.1 can give an overview of action research at work in any organization. Anyone can take the lead. Inviting others to join in on the action moves the endeavor forward. Continuing the initiative with the ideas and commitments of others leads to the transformation of the organization. It is the same organization, but the continuous process of looking at the problem, examining what is known, acquiring knowledge, devising a plan, executing the plan, and repeating the steps as needed brings forth the possibilities—a transformed organization!

STEP-BY-STEP CHECKLIST

Looking at the problem as the first step in L.E.A.D.E.R. dictates a direction for moving toward continuous improvement. Twelve smaller steps to move forward in the process invites and uses collective efficacy to take the other

Figure 13.1   Action Research at Work in the Organization.

steps in moving from problems to possibilities. These twelve steps invite the researcher to begin a process of change.

Step 1. Dissatisfaction with what-is, is the beginning of improvement.
When you find yourself thinking in terms of: "should," "ought to," "why don't they" "how come they never," "they really ought to want to"; "why do I always have to": you are dissatisfied with what-is. That happens in the present state with the realization that this is how it is. You are being cued to think about and write down, if necessary, what the discrepancy is and to make conscious what may be unconscious. In this step, you make conscious the nature of the nagging dissatisfaction.
Step 2. Create a mental or written vision of what the improved condition looks like.
Stephen Covey[5] explained that all things are created twice: once in the imagination and the second time in reality. Step 2 requires the imagined version of how things can be. Consider how the discrepancy of the current state detracts from that vision; what is missing in the picture in the present which must be created?
Step 3. Do a reality check.

Check out your perceptions. Do others in the organization feel the same way as you do? Ask them: what do you think about . . .; do you notice that . . . ? (Be sure to network with colleagues and peers who may have experience with your present situation). This step is done one person at a time, informally, and in a spirit of colleagueship; if the difficulty is one that may be a persistent problem for leaders, teams, front-line workers, be prepared to act rather than react to any negativity and emotion on the part of the respondent.

You are hearing, listening, and welcoming expressions of emotion to reach a stage of descriptive comment; when unpleasant reactions arise, simply acknowledge the strength of the emotion/feelings. This takes a certain amount of personal mastery (lead others by leading self) as you hear things you might not like to hear. Remember, feelings are more influential than thoughts.[6] Also, do not believe everything you think.

Step 4. Think again about the nature of the difficulty.

After gathering perceptions from individuals, the next step is to think again about the nature of the difficulty; begin to consider possible solutions. We have twice as many ears as mouths for a reason. Fullan[7] in his book *Motion Leadership: The Skinny on Becoming Change Savvy* says that savvy leadership involves, among other things, careful entry into the new setting and listening to and learning from those who have been there longer. Reflect on what others have shared. Be open to the new kids on the block, observe those in the ranks, and seek the wisdom of those who have the wisdom to share.

Step 5. Give individuals a chance to hear others in groups.

In this step, give individuals a chance to hear each other in groups small enough to express their own opinions and have time to be heard. Do this informally—during a coffee break, before a meeting, at a lunch gathering. Fullan[8] again recommends that savvy leaders engage in fact-finding and joint problem-solving, carefully (rather than rashly) diagnose the situation, and are enthusiastic, genuine, and sincere about the change circumstances. Savvy leaders give others the opportunity to come together to hear what others are thinking and to share their own thoughts in a non-threatening way.

Step 6. Use the information from the groups to generate your own solution.

After letting individuals hear each other in small groups, use this information to begin generating in your own mind or on paper, a solution that will produce in the future, what is lacking in the present. If "what-is" is not what you would like it to be, your challenge, your task, your responsibility, is to create the conditions that will produce in the future, what is lacking in the present!

Step 7. Another round of asking individuals.

In this step begin another round of informally asking individuals, one at a time, in a manner that evokes thought and comment and sharing, what they think about these possible solutions. Once again, you must be willing to accept negativity and emotional expression depending on the nature of the problem. Remember to use your two ears more frequently than your one mouth.

Be enthusiastic, genuine, and sincere about the change circumstances that can be considered. Obtain buy-in for what needs fixing to move from the problem to the possibility. Then with this new information, develop a credible plan for making that fix.

Step 8. Write a proposal plan.

After this round of informal data gathering, you can write up the plan you propose for dealing with the change you would like to achieve. You are taking a step from data to decision making. Data includes feelings, emotions, as well as stats. For instance, 1777 is data—numbers unrelated to anything when viewed merely as data. However, when you add information to that data—$17.77, the picture changes. When examining what you know such as the cost of the Screwdriver Pen Pocket Multi-Tool By Edge-Works from Amazon for $13.00, you have even more knowledge. This knowledge leads to a decision—buy it!

Step 9. Listen one more time to each other.

At this point, it is time for the staff to *hear from each other again.* Now that you know what each person thinks and feels, you are prepared to deal with whatever dissent, discussion, etc. may come up, and you are in a position to call upon individuals to present other viewpoints. Explore the importance of building the organization by focusing on the executive and senior leaders, project teams, front-line employees, managers, and supervisors. The key is enabling staff to learn continuously and to hear each other. This process allows the organization to work together, interdependently, to analyze and impact professional practice in order to improve individual and collective results.

Step 10. Present a written plan.

At this meeting, the written plan is presented, not for approval but for discussion, adjustment, revision, rewriting. The result needs to include whole group thinking and contribution. Once the plan has been decided upon—with a view to enlarging the length of the continuum of opposing values where the individual can be comfortable—strategies are selected to put the plan into action. This step may take more than one meeting and may involve subcommittee work. Eventually, a pilot program is chosen.

Step 11. Continuous evaluation of the change process.

Evaluation is constant. Each day, you speak to each person to see "how it's going." At subsequent staff meetings, everyone "counts" progress; those who are unsuccessful share what has to be avoided; those who are successful share what has worked. You continually devise strategies for using talent and building on strengths. Fullan[9] describes this as connecting peers with the purpose for the change. Purposeful peer interaction within the organization is crucial. Learning and achievement increase substantially when peers work in learning communities supported by a focus on improvement.

Step 12. Celebrate progress.

When positive progress (not perfection!) is evident, CELEBRATE! Institutionalize the procedures proven successful by the pilot; eliminate those elements that militate against progress. Incremental celebrations of progress enhance morale, identify the strategies that should be used more frequently, and give greater sight to the ultimate goal. When the celebration is held off until the end—or until perfection is reached, change becomes an event to be celebrated rather than a process that happens and a PROCESS that should be celebrated.

As you go along, use this handout (table 13.2) to list your own change topic and the steps you might take to create the change you wish to see.

As Gandhi says, be the change you want! Think about what that means for you first, then for others who are involved in the desired change.

ACTION RESEARCH AS A GROWTH
MINDSET FOR CHANGE

Since the publication of Carol Dweck's[10] *Mindset, the New Psychology of Success*, consideration of how individuals approach life based on their

Table 13.2   Handout for Creating Your Own Steps to Change

	Steps to Change	Steps to Create the Change
1	Dissatisfaction with what-is, is the beginning of improvement.	
2	Create a mental or written vision of what the improved condition looks like.	
3	Do a reality check.	
4	Think again about the nature of the difficulty.	
5	Give individuals a chance to hear others in groups.	
6	Use the information from the groups to generate your own solution.	
7	Another round of asking individuals.	
8	Write a proposal plan.	
9	Listen one more time to each other.	
10	Present a written plan.	
11	Continuous evaluation of the change process.	
12	Celebrate.	

beliefs that are fixed or growth-minded has flooded the market. Dweck explains that the fixed mindset personality assumes that character, intelligence, and creative ability are givens that cannot be changed in any meaningful way and that success is determined by inherent intelligence. In the fixed mindset, being smart equates with striving for success and avoiding failure at all costs. The growth mindset, on the other hand, thrives on challenge and views failure as a springboard for growth and stretching existing abilities.

The success or failure of an organization is heavily influenced by the mindset of its leaders and the relationships of its workers. Jim Collins[11] in his research on the great organizations found that great companies were willing to admit mistakes or change tactics and were guided by facts and information that benefitted the whole company. Jack Welch used a growth mindset as he brought success to GE by visiting the company's factories, speaking with workers, and learning from others whenever he could. Welch credited his accomplishments to involving others, asking feedback from employees, asking what they liked and disliked about GE, and what they thought could be improved. Collins found the greatness of GE and other companies was in the growth mindset of its leaders and its members.

In reviewing Dweck's[12] research on growth mindset, key words and phrases surface: belief, challenge, sharing the process, learning, opportunity, effort, success, discipline. Action research mirrors many of these same words and phrases. Action research begins with seeing a possibility.

The vision to possibility includes a belief that one can step out of the current situation and believe in the possibility to achieve. Action research begins with dissatisfaction with what-is and embracing a challenge as an opportunity. The process is more important than the end result. The learning is in the process and does not depend on the approval of others. The fixed mindset questions: Will this be good enough? Will someone else do it better? Growth mindset has a sense of purpose: a sense there is something greater than yourself, the organization, and more important than competition with others. Purpose is the strongest driver in action research. Purpose is what brings action to the research.

Actions are what matter. Doing something smart or in a smart way is far better than being smart. Approaching problems with interest and a desire to learn is irreplaceable. Mistakes along the way are opportunities to change an approach. Growth is more important than speed and examining what is known and acquiring knowledge in the process takes effort which is the path to mastery.

Hard work, criticism, room for improvement become the tools to possibility and are not signs of failure. Action research is not an all-or-nothing approach to continuous improvement. One works harder to achieve what one wants and envisions as possible. Learning from one's own mistakes and the mistakes of others are valuable learning resources in action research. Taking risks, even as others watch, expands opportunity. Without taking the risk, opportunity diminishes.

Remember to celebrate the success of others. Those successes, whether large or small, are an inspiration to the whole organization. Organizations that see senior leaders and executives, project teams, front-line employees, managers, and supervisors as colleagues and inspiration can see much further than viewing them as competitors. This approach creates honest and strong working relationships among the organization and enhances everyone's own chances for growth.

Begin with the end in mind. Consider what is disconnected from the possible reality. Examine the small but necessary steps to change. Take the steps, develop the growth mindset of the organization. Move from problems to possibilities.

NOTES

1. Covey, S. R. (1991). *The seven habits of highly effective people.* Provo, UT: Covey Leadership Center.

2. Scott, E. (2020). The expectation vs. the reality trap: Are you being robbed of your happiness? https://www.verywellmind.com/expectation-vs-reality-trap-4570968

3. Creasey, T. (n.d.) *Change as a process* [online]. https://blog.prosci.com/change-is-a-process

4. Creasey, *Change as a process.*

5. Covey, *The seven habits.*

6. Kotter, J. P. (2008). *A sense of urgency.* Harvard Business Press.

7. Fullan, M. (2010). *Motion leadership: The skinny on becoming change savvy.* Corwin Press.

8. Fullan, *Motion leadership.*

9. Fullan, *Motion leadership.*

10. Dweck, C. S. (2006). *Mindset: The new psychology of success.* Ballantine Books

11. Collins, J. (2001). *Good to great.* New York: HarperCollins Inc.

12. Dweck, *Mindset.*

Chapter 14

What Comes Next?

Be willing to share your blessings.
The only riches that last are the ones that are given away.

—David Khalil

An essential element in action research is sharing the action research study. This chapter will address questions from chapter 7, "Look at the Problem," to assist the researcher to present—share—the results of the research. Questions such as "For whom is the problem a problem?" and "Why hasn't the problem been solved up to this point?" will help the researcher determine the audience who needs to hear about the research. The chapter will include suggestions for ways to present the research.

NO END IN SIGHT

The biggest sigh of relief at the end of a research project is that the research is finally over, done, completed, submitted, and accepted. In action research, the end is another beginning. Action research does not end with a finished product, but as often stated in this book, the end is a part of the ongoing process to continuous improvement. There is no end, but rather the next beginning.

Unlike scientific research seeking a final finding, action research triggers additional action. The researcher who is intimately connected to the research engages in the ongoing process of research and improvement. The process helps the researcher think deeply about what has been researched, what the findings revealed, how the research and findings were significant for the researcher and the organization, and how the research contributes to learning beyond the organization researched. Preparing the work for public consumption requires another layer of scrutiny and validity to the whole process. Reflection is a major component of action research.

CAN YOU SURVIVE ACTION RESEARCH IN YOUR OWN ORGANIZATION?

Action research is about improving practice by undertaking action and studying that action as it unfolds. Action research is collaborative. The researcher is a member of the organization and reaches out to other members of the organization as co-researchers. The action researcher is seeking to attain personal goals and accomplish organizational transformation.

The role of the action researcher as an insider in the research is messy. Brookfield[1] describes this role as impostorship, cultural suicide, lost innocence, roadrunning, and community. Anyone attempting to study the inner workings of their own organization goes out on a limb, risking knowing something that others know more about, censuring friends and colleagues, facing unwanted ambiguities, moving two steps forward only to move one step back! However, discovering critical friends and reflective mirrors who confirm the insider researcher is not alone in the process, who endorse the findings, the dissonance, help the insider researcher make sense of the whole experience.

The action researcher has a unique role. The researcher is an active member of the organization under study while attempting to be the change agent. The researcher has the opportunity to enhance practice while simultaneously making it even better. The researcher is also challenged to be objective, ethical, and moral in the action research process. The researcher not only conducts the research but implements the change studied.

One of the most important actions in action research, particularly for the researcher, is reflective practice. Raelin describes reflective practice as:

> periodically stepping back to ponder the meaning of what has recently transpired to ourselves and to others in our immediate environment. It illuminates what the self and others have experienced, providing a basis for future action. In particular, it privileges the process of inquiry, leading to an understanding of experiences that may have been overlooked in practice.[2]

Reflective practice, while recognizing the importance of private reflection, promotes the review of others while opening the interpretation and evaluation of the plans and actions of the research for public scrutiny. This is done throughout the process, not just at the end! Reflective practice is not the modus operandi in most organizations. The boss, CEO, executive is not interested in thinking about solutions, but rather wants action.

While the brain can handle 50,000 or more thoughts a day, when the individual encounters a problem at work, the individual tends to go no farther than the *solution database*—to find the standard answer—the solution or assumption that has worked in the past. This limits possibilities to experiences of the researcher. When the researcher shares the problem with co-researchers, this community of reflective practitioners now have multiple ideas that can be processed as a group, with collective intelligence.

Organizations that inspire reflection generate new ways of coping with change. A reflective culture makes it possible for members of an organization to constantly challenge without fear of retaliation.[3] These challenges result in moving from problems to possibilities. This makes action research in an organization not only possible but also profitable.

WHAT TO REFLECT ON IN ACTION RESEARCH

The first level of reflection in action research is what the researcher researched. Reflection is the opportunity to sort through one's thinking, decide on what is significant, and plan next steps. Because action research is recursive, reflection on what has been researched is a constant in the process. One of the preliminary questions in looking at the problem (chapter 7) was: *Why has the problem not been solved up to this point?* As the research unfolds, the answer to this question becomes more obvious as the researcher and co-researchers reflect collaboratively.

A hometown furniture store prided itself on being *Your Hometown Headquarters.* Serving customers in a 200-mile radius, they limited their customer base and developed a philosophy of fairness to the customer. The lofty belief and philosophy attracted and retained loyal customers. While the customers were generally pleased with their products, an ongoing issue with delivery caused repeated problems. More than once, the furniture was delivered on time, but at least one item was not the item ordered. To be fair to the customer, the company offered to leave the wrong item until the correct item was delivered.

This issue, while a temporary inconvenience for the customer, became a financial drain for the company. The wrong piece of furniture was now used and could not be sold at market value. If this had been a single event, it may have gone unnoticed. But upon review, this was happening about once a month. Why was this problem not yet solved?

The delivery foreman became the researcher in this situation. He not only looked at the mistakes but also considered what happened to make most of the deliveries timely and correct. He considered more than the standard database of solutions. He engaged his team in the research: 96 percent of orders were correct and timely; 100 percent of orders were delivered during the workweek; 100 percent of the mistaken furniture were love seats; 78 percent of the orders that resulted in mistakes were made on Friday afternoons.

Why had the problem not been solved? The data collection revealed that loveseats ordered on Friday afternoons were the targeted mistakes. Further research required investigation of who was taking the orders, why loveseats were the mistakes, and what happened on Friday afternoons that caused these errors. Collaborative research and reflection caused the team to increase diligence with orders—particularly loveseats—on Friday afternoons.

Another level of reflective practice includes what the findings of the research reveal. In the case of the furniture store, the findings revealed that loveseats ordered Friday afternoons could be a problem. But the data also revealed that 96 percent of orders were correct and that errors in furniture orders placed Mondays through Thursdays and on the weekends were flawless.

Without blaming anyone, the foreman and his team compared the ordering process on Friday afternoons with all the other days. They also examined orders of loveseats and found that fewer loveseats were ordered on Fridays than any other day of the week.

Fewer orders resulted in less knowledge about the loveseats, less familiarity with stock numbers and delivery routines, and limited expertise on loveseats of salespersons who worked the floors on Friday afternoons. New inventory was delivered on Friday mornings and the weekend salespersons (the Friday–Sunday employees) had limited time to become familiar with the new inventory. Reflective practice resulted in needed changes.

The significance of the research for both the researcher and the organization resulted in making some basic changes. While the delivery of new inventory on Friday mornings could not easily be changed, a process could be put in place for creating expertise for loveseat sales representatives.

Loveseats became the new specialty on Friday afternoons. Two salespersons became the loveseat specialists, focusing on all that needed to be known about available loveseats. They received training, the first hour of their shift on Fridays included a review of the new inventory and the available loveseats in stock, and they became part of the advertising campaign for the Friday afternoon specials on loveseats. Within two months, mistakes on loveseat deliveries were eliminated, the company no longer had to deal with used furniture, and the sales of loveseats increased.

While this was good news for the furniture company, what significance could these findings have for other departments in the organization or for other organizations? In the executive leadership monthly team meetings, the loveseat revenue increase did not go unnoticed. When any department makes a positive change, the change benefits the whole organization. Proactive organizations pay greater attention to positive changes than focusing on what is not working. This type of reflection addresses the question: *For whom is the problem a problem?*

Before actually researching this issue, the company recognized they were losing revenue due to the accumulation of used furniture. What was less obvious was the focus on loveseats as the issue. Furthermore, the company did not see a need for experts in types of furniture for reviewing sales profits on certain days of the week, and for involving salespersons as part of the advertising group. The problem was a problem for the customer, the delivery team, the weekend salespersons, and the organization as a whole because of lost revenue. Collective efficacy changed the problem to a possibility.

In addition to sharing the findings of the research within the delivery department, the findings impacted the sales and marketing departments. Findings were also shared at national trade shows and conferences that include informative seminars and insight into today's social media world, with a focus on forecasting and planning for the future of the furniture industry. These events provide an opportunity to network with top retail, manufacturing, transportation, and media executives and thus share findings well beyond *Your Hometown Headquarters.*

For some, doing action research in your own organization can be exciting, fulfilling, and an opportunity for growth both personally and in the organization. For others, it may be Brookfield's[4] tales from the dark side with a high potential for self-destruction. For those committed to leadership in action, collaborative efficacy, continuous improvement, and organizational transformation, action research is leadership moving from problems to unimagined possibilities.

MEDIUM FOR SHARING FINDINGS

The medium the action researcher chooses to present findings will depend on the audience. In Chapter 12, consideration was made for the audiences who would receive the findings of a study. Sharing findings even within the organization will have its limits as not everyone will have the same level of interest in the findings nor be impacted by the findings.

A major component of action research is sharing the findings. How to share those findings becomes a question for the researcher and for the organization that supports the group efficacy approach toward continuous improvement.

Consider how the study could be replicated in another context. Think about other organizations with similar problems and craft an oral or written presentation that will provide needed details to use the same surveys, data collection methods, or background knowledge. In most instances of action research with organizations, it will not be possible to replicate the study exactly. In sharing the study, select the components that can be used by organizations with similar products, processes, or customers. With these intended audiences, it will be easier to determine what information will be most helpful to them.

Another consideration in sharing the study, be sure the evidence used to generate claims or actions is clearly documented. In the furniture store study, the actual data collected on profitable sales would not have allowed the organization to see the full picture. Investigating the errors and comparing those errors to what worked well provided a more significant finding about the Friday sales slump. Additionally, sharing the specific actions taken by the organization—training, inventory reviews, marketing strategies—allows other audiences the opportunity to consider differing challenges.

Sharing how the action taken was tracked during the research process is often helpful for other organizations. Once the furniture store rectified the Friday issues—and there were several other issues related to Fridays—the low sales of loveseats, new inventory, weekend workers—their results changed. Organizations want to know how this happens so that they can consider the actions they will need to take and also have a sense of how long this may take, what additional data will be needed to track the actions, and whether the efforts taken are worth the intended results. Sharing the information about success that encourages others is a perfect example of information that contributes to developing collective efficacy.

One more consideration in sharing the study and its findings is the accessibility of the information with one who is also affected by the problem. Sharing the study and its findings incorporates the consumer into the organization. Consumers may be executives, project teams, or those who are producers or who maintain the organization. Each of these will have a different need for the information from the study. Plans for making these findings accessible will require considerable planning and distribution.

Additionally, consumers will be those beyond the organization. Making decisions about accessibility of the study and the findings will require corporate decisions regarding the sharing. The more sensitive the issue under study, the more limited will be the accessibility. With studies that have a more common process or product, the sharing is often more generous.

When the audience has been determined, the format for sharing the study and its findings is easier to plan. Within-house sharing can be in Board Meetings, department updates, organizational publications, or even in a formalized presentation. While the same formats are possible for those beyond the organization, an invitation to share the study will generally be a mode for initiating the sharing. Other public sharing can include newspaper articles, magazine articles, and even journal submissions.

In addition to sharing the action research through journal submissions, networks for sharing action research ideas, results, studies, and other resources exist. The Center for Collaborative Action Research (CCAR) shares through its wikispace. *The Collaborative Action Research Network*,[5] an international network, shares online and paid membership resources.

POSTER SESSION SHARING

Finding the ideal format for presenting their research can be as daunting as taking the first steps in action research. Rowell, Polush, Riel, and Bruewer[6] (2015) describe this involvement:

Making decisions about involvement in action research carries certain risks. It involves interrogating one's thinking and deciding actively to change established self-perceptions and personal and professional habits to move into the future, recognizing that action researchers are responsible for their decisions and the consequences of their decisions.

Specific action research practices are informed by researchers' values that carry hope for the future including the procedural principle of democracy and insights from the most advanced social theories of the day. The action researcher, like all researchers, is expected to share research findings as part of the process of knowledge creation. Action researchers also expect to have those findings scrutinized by other professionals, including professionals whose knowledge and belief systems may vary markedly from those of the action researchers.

One format that is helpful for those who are new to presenting research is the poster format. The purpose of the poster is to display graphically the highlights of the action research, to make learning visible, and to share learning. Often poster sessions follow a set format known as IMRaD (introduction, methods, results, and discussion). The format of the poster is three or four columns on a physical poster board large enough to be seen from a reasonable distance away.

Because posters in the social sciences and humanities tend to be text-heavy, the researcher may need to change text to graphics. The poster should include tables, lists, and figures to present data. The poster should use short sentences or phrases bulleted into lists to capture large amounts of information. Persuade the audience by selecting message headings suggested by *Cornell vs. Harvard in Note taking* rather than the common nondescript headings such as introduction, methods, and results.

Select colors purposefully. Text and background colors need to contrast for easy reading. Background colors for different sections of your poster should be related. Choose fonts that are easy to read from a distance.

A sans serif font (the kind of font that does not have feet) is a better choice for posters—especially if the audience is three to five feet away from the poster. *Arial* font has no feet and is cleaner and clearer than serif fonts such as *Times New Roman*. Font size makes a difference with posters.

Titles should be ninety points or higher and only about six to eight words; headings should be 36–48 points and about three words; and text should be about 30–36 points. *The Cain Project in Engineering and Professional Communication*[7] is one of many resources that provides templates for poster presentations and other helpful directives for creating and presenting posters.

Most posters can be created from PowerPoint templates, an easy way to design a poster because much of the formatting is contained within the poster. Selecting a template can be quite easy and templates are also available in Microsoft Word and Publisher. Templates are free downloads at the Microsoft website.

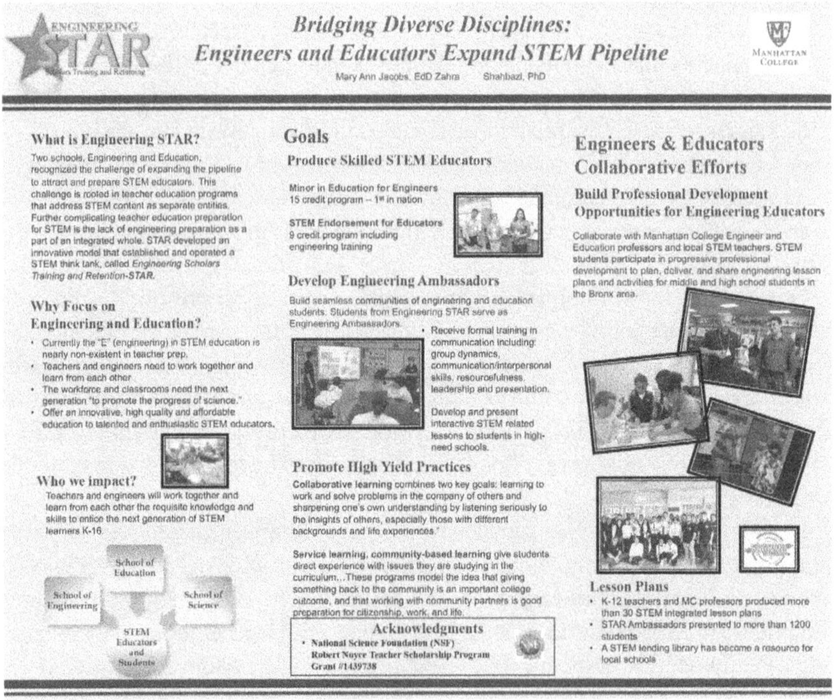

Figure 14.1   Three-Column Poster Presentation.

Once the template is downloaded, the researcher determines how the information from the action research should be displayed. A common error among new and nearly new action research presenters is to try to condense an action research paper into a poster template. The researcher should overcome the temptation to copy paragraphs directly from the research paper and paste it into the poster—thus giving the text-heavy appearance to the poster. Figure 14.1 is a sample of a three-column poster that includes text and graphics.

POSTER PRESENTATION

Making the poster is just the first part of the presentation. Presenting the information in the poster is even more important. The goal of a professional poster presentation is clearly and concisely to lead the audience through the study in about five minutes.

Poster presentations are generally held in large conference rooms with ample space for poster displays. Unlike a conference presentation, several posters can be on display simultaneously, so the presenter is generally not the only one talking. The audience moves around the room, stopping at posters that interest them.

Presenters have only a few minutes to provide the audience with an overview of the research. The purpose of the poster is to give a visual image of the information that the presenter is making. The presenter should never read from the poster. The presenter knows the research so well that the poster provides the visual for the audience, and the presenter uses the poster to direct the attention of the audience. The poster, however, should be able to stand on its own, so the audience can understand the research even if the presenter is not there.

Think of the presentation as what the researcher would be able to tell someone about the research in a two-minute elevator ride—the elevator speech! Stand to the side of the poster to present the information to the audience. Greet the audience but then give them time to read the poster. Engage them in the research once they have had time to read the poster, or if they ask a question. Speak loudly enough to be heard by all those gathered around the poster and slowly enough to appear relaxed, knowledgeable, and not rushed.

Adhere to the suggested time frame for the presentation. Begin with the major focus for the action research—generally the problem that was addressed. Take the viewers through each part of the research. Use the L.E.A.D.E.R. format to present the research. Practice ahead of time, preferably with a real audience not familiar with the research. Be prepared to respond to questions but be honest if you do not know the answer to a question. Thank the audience for coming to the poster presentation.

The above guidelines are formulated for making poster presentations at conferences but can also be used for making presentations to all audiences. A poster is easy to transport from place to place and requires minimal time to set up. If a poster is designed for multiple audiences, the content of the poster needs to reflect each audience. If the L.E.A.D.E.R. format is followed in the design of the poster, this format can easily be adapted to different audiences with the same effectiveness.

NEXT STEPS TOWARD CONTINUOUS IMPROVEMENT

Action research is never finished. Whether the problem of the research has been solved or not, next steps will need to be taken. Sometimes those steps include revisiting the original problem and determining why a proposed solution did not work. Other times the steps will include moving on to incorporate changes made through the research. Completing an action research process is often the impetus for starting the next action research project. Success begets success and deepens the conviction that together, "we can do this!"

In all circumstances, learning needs to be made visible. First—and sometimes only—within the organization. However, sharing learning made visible is an equally important imperative. Learning, like the action research process, is collegial and interdependent, not an independent or isolated project. The research needs to be shared with other practitioners who may be facing similar situations. If the research stops with the researcher, the learning terminates prematurely. Action research requires action and public dissemination of the findings.

An important goal of action research is solving problems. Solving problems is a leadership function. Leaders solve problems collaboratively. They work with other leaders who are willing to lead up. The anticipated outcome is a better organization. The leadership mindset for action research collaborators is thinking that problems are gateways to future possibilities.

NOTES

1. Brookfield, S. (1994). Tales from the dark side: A phenomenography of adult critical reflection. *International Journal of Lifelong Education, 13*(3), 203–216.

2. Raelin, J. A. (2002). 'I Don't Have Time to Think!' (vs. The art of reflective practice). *Reflections, 4*(1), 66–79.

3. Raelin, 'I Don't Have Time to Think!'

4. Brookfield, Tales from the dark side.

5. CARN. (2019). *The collaborative action research network.* CARN-ALARA Conference. Imagine tomorrow: Practitioner learning for the Future. https://carn-alara2019.org/about-carn

6. Rowell, L., Polush, E., Riel, M., and Bruewer, A. (2015) *Action researchers' perspectives about the distinguishing characteristics of action research: A Delphi and learning circles mixed-methods study.* Access online at http://www.tandfonline.com/doi/abs/10.1080/09650792.2014.990987#.VPlW0IH-Oxw

7. *Cain project in engineering and professional communication.* (2003). Rice University. Retrieved at http://www.owlnet.rice.edu/~cainproj//ih_posters.html

Index

About the Authors

Mary Ann Jacobs, scc, is an associate professor in education and leadership at Manhattan College, Bronx, New York. She has been an educator at every level—teaching kindergarten through postgraduate courses in leadership, assessment, curriculum, technology, and instructional design and delivery. She prepares education majors to become teachers for middle and high-school students. Her research interests include action research, STEM education, brain compatible instruction, and effective middle schools. She may be contacted at maryann.jacobs@manhattan.edu.

Remigia Kushner, csj, is a professor of education and the director of educational leadership in the Graduate Education Program at Manhattan College, Bronx, New York. She has experience as a classroom teacher, administrator, district and associate superintendent, educational consultant, author, and national speaker. She serves on the Commissioner's Advisory Council for Nonpublic Schools for New York State and on the Educational Excellence Network. Her research interests include professional development, continuous improvement of teaching and learning, and reflective leadership practice. She may be contacted at sr.remigia.kushner@manhattan.edu.

Jacobs and Kushner were co-authors of *How Can You Become the Boss?: From Personal Mastery to Organizational Transformation* at Rowman & Littlefield.